The Class Struggle

ALSO IN THE NORTON LIBRARY

THE MARXIAN REVOLUTIONARY IDEA
by *Robert C. Tucker*   N539

The Class Struggle

(ERFURT PROGRAM)

By KARL KAUTSKY

TRANSLATED BY WILLIAM E. BOHN

With an Introduction by Robert C. Tucker

The Norton Library

W · W · NORTON & COMPANY · INC ·
NEW YORK

Published simultaneously in Canada by
George J. McLeod Limited, Toronto

Books That Live

The Norton imprint on a book means that in the publisher's
estimation it is a book not for a single season but for the years.
W. W. Norton & Company, Inc.

Copyright © 1971 by W. W. Norton & Company, Inc.

SBN 393 00567 4

PRINTED IN THE UNITED STATES OF AMERICA
1 2 3 4 5 6 7 8 9 0

CONTENTS.

CONTENTS.

INTRODUCTION

This book is one of the minor classics of Marxist thought. It was written in 1892 as a general statement of the articles of belief of the Social Democratic Party of Germany (S.P.D.), then the largest and most influential Marxist party in Europe. Its author, Karl Kautsky, was editor of the party's theoretical journal *Neue Zeit* and—save for the aged but still active Friedrich Engels—the foremost theoretician of German Marxism.

Kautsky was the chief architect of the new program adopted by the S.P.D. at its congress in Erfurt in 1891.[1] The Erfurt program supplanted the program adopted at the conference in Gotha in 1875, at which the followers of Marx and those of Ferdinand Lassalle combined to form a united German socialist labor party. For the benefit of the party leaders, Marx had penned a series of sharply critical marginal notes on the draft Gotha program, attacking its Lassallean features. Engels, with Kautsky's help, published Marx's notes in *Neue Zeit* in 1891 in an effort to ensure that the new program would be drawn up in the spirit of orthodox Marxism, which it was.[2] The twelve years of repression endured by the party between

1. Carl E. Schorske, *German Social Democracy 1905–1917. The Development of the Great Schism* (Cambridge, Mass., 1955), 4.
2. *Ibid.* For the text of Marx's critical notes, see his "Critique of the Gotha Program" in *The Marx-Engels Reader* (New York, 1971).

1878 and 1890 under Bismarck's anti-socialist laws had greatly helped to prepare the way psychologically, however, for this outcome.

The new Erfurt program consisted of a theoretical part and a practical section setting forth the party's minimum program: the demands for reform that could be realized without revolutionary overthrow of the existing order. After the Erfurt congress, Kautsky undertook to amplify the theoretical part in a series of commentaries aimed at making the party's official views comprehensible and cogent to the broad public. What was needed, he wrote in his preface to the first German edition, was a sort of "catechism of Social Democracy," something deeper and more detailed than the available popular pamphlets on Marxism and yet not so specialized as the principal theoretical monographs of Marx and Engels themselves. The result was the present volume, which is here reprinted in the somewhat condensed English translation by William E. Bohn, first published in the United States in 1910.

The first three chapters of the book, comprising less than half its total bulk, summarize the economic argumentation of *Capital*. Essentially this material is a systematization of the views of Marx and Engels on the developmental dialectic of capitalist society. Chapters IV and V, however, give us Marxism in its end-of-the-century Social Democratic extension. Although with many references to the founders, Kautsky here elaborates their teachings according to the experience and dictates of the socialist movement of his time. His chapter on "The Commonwealth of the

Future" is at once an attempted envisagement of socialism in the frame of the modern nation-state and a frank work of advocacy of socialism against the arguments of its critics, and his concluding chapter on "The Class Struggle" sets forth the S.P.D.'s political strategy.

Kautsky's advocacy of the socialist transformation of society is notably moderate in tone. Seeking to be persuasive to the unconvinced as well as the party faithful, it is devoid of the spirit of radical alienation from existing society that stamps so many of the writings of Marx. Clearly, this is the presentation of a Social Democratic political leader who hopes to see his party come to power by peaceful parliamentary means and carry through a socio-economic revolution, of which he says: "It is by no means necessary that it be accompanied with violence and bloodshed" (p. 91). In this connection, it should be noted that Marx's famous revolutionary phrase "dictatorship of the proletariat" appears nowhere in these pages. Kautsky expects the proletariat to "exert all its energy to increase the power of parliaments in relation to other departments of government and to swell to the utmost its own parliamentary representation," looking to the socialist party's "conquest of the government in the interest of the class which it represents" (pp. 188, 189).

Such was the S.P.D.'s political doctrine. While continuing to profess the classical Marxist belief in the coming revolutionary breakdown of the bourgeois order, it was practicing the politics of democratic socialism. Here were the roots of the great clash that occurred between Kautsky and Lenin in the aftermath of the Russian Revolution. Kautsky condemned the Bolshevik leader and his party for betraying the Marxist commitment to democracy by setting up a single-party dictatorship resting on force and violence, while Lenin assailed "the renegade Kautsky" for betraying Marxism by renouncing in both theory and practice its core and "essence"—the teaching on the dictatorship of the proletariat.[3] The controversy between the two men and their Marxisms sealed the split between Communism and Social Democracy.

Yet the reader of Kautsky's commentaries on the Erfurt program will find many passages that illuminate the almost reverential respect that the younger Lenin had felt for the orthodox Kautsky of that time as a Marxist teacher. Thus Kautsky discusses the relation between the socialist party and the working-class movement in a manner that certainly influenced the views Lenin was to express in works like *What Is To Be Done?* In two pages (pp. 103–104) he sets forth the theory of imperialist expansionism and war that underlies Lenin's later treatise on *Imperialism: The Highest Stage of Capitalism*. Elsewhere he decries the "children's disease" of leftist extremism that threatens every "young" socialist movement,

3. Karl Kautsky, *The Dictatorship of the Proletariat* (Ann Arbor, 1964); Lenin, *The Proletarian Revolution and the Renegade Kautsky,* in *Selected Works* (Moscow, 1946–1947), Vol. II. For a fuller discussion of the conflicting Leninist and Kautskyan interpretations of Marxism, see R. Tucker, *The Marxian Revolutionary Idea* (New York, 1969), chapters 3 and 6.

prefiguring Lenin's work of nearly three decades later on *Left-Wing Communism: A Children's Disease*. And his concluding section on "The International Character of the Socialist Movement" was doubtless one of the doctrinal sources of the uncompromising socialist internationalism of Lenin.

Kautsky's "catechism" more than fulfilled the historical role he foresaw for it. It became one of the formative influences on the understanding of Marxism then and later. It came out in many German editions in the early years of the century and was translated into various foreign languages. The editor of a Russian translation published in the Soviet Union in 1959 had this to say of the work, along with some criticisms: "Much here has retained its value to the present time. Kautsky managed to give a popular exposition of the most important theoretical tenents of Marxism." [4] Which was to say that there is more than a little in common between the orthodox Marxism of Kautsky's commentaries and that professed by Soviet Communism in our time.

ROBERT C. TUCKER

Princeton, N.J.
January 1971

---

4. K. Kautsky, *Erfurtskaia programma (Kommentarii k printsipial'noi chasti)* (Moscow, 1959), 4. The author of the Soviet preface is N. Shevtsov.

The Class Struggle.

I. THE PASSING OF SMALL PRODUCTION.

1. Small Production and Private Property.

The program adopted by the German Social Democracy at Erfurt in 1891 divides itself into two parts. In the first place it outlines the fundamental principles on which Socialism is based, and in the second it enumerates the demands which the Social Democracy makes of present day society. The first part tells what Socialists believe; the second how they propose to make their belief effective.

We shall concern ourselves only with the first of these parts. This again separates itself into three divisions: (1) an analysis of present day society and its development; (2) the objects of the Social Democracy; (3) the means which are to lead to the realization of these objects.

The first section of the program reads as follows: "Production on a small scale is based on the ownership of the means of production by the laborer. The economic development of bourgeois society leads necessarily to the overthrow of this form of production. It separates the worker from his tools and changes him into a propertyless proletarian. The means of production become more and more the monopoly of a comparatively small number of capitalists and landholders.

"Along with this monopolizing of the means of production goes the crowding out and scattering of small production, the development of the tool into the machine, and a marvelous increase in the productivity of labor. But all the advantages of this transformation are monopolized by capitalists and landholders. For the proletariat and the disappearing middle class—the small business men and farmers—it means increasing uncertainty of subsistence; it means misery, oppression, servitude, degradation and exploitation.

"Forever greater grows the number of proletarians, more gigantic the army of superfluous laborers, and sharper the opposition between exploiters and exploited. The class-struggle between the bourgeoisie and proletariat is the common mark of all industrial countries; it divides modern society into two opposing camps and the warfare between them constantly increases in bitterness.

"The abyss between propertied and propertyless is further widened by industrial crises. These have their causes in the capitalist system and, as the system develops, naturally occur on an increasing scale. They make universal uncertainty the normal condition of society and so prove that our power of production has got beyond our control, that private ownership of the means of production has become irreconcilable with their effective use and complete development."

* * *

Many a man thinks he has given proof of wisdom when he says, "There is nothing new under the sun." There is nothing more false. Modern science shows that nothing is stationary, that in society, just as in external nature, a continuous development is discoverable.

On the nature of this social development is based the theory of Socialism. No one can understand the one without study of the other.

We know that primitive man lived, like the animals, on whatever nature happened to offer. But in the course of time he began to devise tools. He became fisher, hunter, herdsman, finally farmer and craftsman. This development was constantly accelerated, until today we can see it going on before our eyes and mark its stages. And still there are those who solemnly proclaim that there is nothing new under the sun.

A people's way of getting a living depends on its means of production—on the nature of its tools and raw materials. But men have never carried on production separately; always, on the contrary, in larger or smaller societies. And the varying forms of these societies have depended on the manner of production. The development of society, therefore, corresponds to a development of the manner of production.

The forms of society and the relations of its members are intimately connected with the forms of property which it maintains. Hand in hand with the development of production goes a development of property. So long as labor was performed with comparatively simple tools which each laborer could possess, it went without saying that he owned the product of his toil. But as the means of production have changed, this notion of property right has passed away.

We shall examine the course of development which has brought this about.

2. Commodities and Capital.

The beginnings of capitalist society are to be found in agriculture and handicraft.

Originally the agricultural family satisfied all of its own needs. It produced all the food, clothing and tools for its own members and built its own house. It produced as much as it needed and no more. With the advance in the methods of farming, however, it came about that more was produced than enough to satisfy the immediate needs of the family. This placed the family in a position to purchase weapons, tools or articles of luxury, which it could not produce itself. Through this exchange products became commodities.

A commodity is a product designed for exchange. The wheat the farmer produces for his own consumption is not a commodity; the wheat he produces to sell is a commodity. Selling is nothing more nor less than trading a commodity for another which is acceptable to all, gold, for example.

Now the craftsman working independently is a producer of commodities from the beginning. He does not sell merely his surplus products; production for sale is his main purpose.

Exchange of commodities implies two conditions: first, a division of social labor; second, private ownership of the things exchanged. The more this division develops and the more private property increases in extent and importance, the more general becomes production for exchange. This leads naturally to the appearance of a new trade; buying and selling becomes a business. Those engaged in it make their living by selling dearer than they buy. This does not mean that they control prices absolutely. The price of a commodity depends finally on its exchange value. The value of a commodity, however, is determined by the amount of labor generally required to produce it. The price of a commodity, nevertheless, seldom coincides exactly with its value; it is determined by the conditions of the market more than by the conditions of production—primarily by the relation of supply and demand.

The farmer or craftsman buys for consumption, the tradesman buys to sell. Now money used for this latter purpose is capital. One cannot say of any commodity or sum of money that by its very nature it is capital. That depends on the use to which it is put. The tobacco a merchant buys to sell is capital; that which he buys to smoke is not.

The original form of capital is merchant's capital. Almost equally old is interest-bearing capital, the profits of which are in the form of interest. As soon as these forms of capital have been developed, private property becomes something quite different from what it was in the beginning. Defenders of the present system try to distract attention from this aspect of property by talking constantly of the forms necessary to the beginnings of society. They attempt to prevent our seeing any difference between the ownership of a home and the ownership of a branch of industry.

At the stage of economic development now under discussion the income of the craftsman or laborer depends somewhat on his industry and skill. But it can never go beyond a fixed limit. That of the tradesman, however, is determined only by the amount of his capital. The possibilities of labor are limited; those of capital are unlimited.

So we have here a condition that would naturally lead to social development. We started with a society in which each owned certain means of production; in which, therefore, the individuals were approximately equal. The natural limitations of the income from labor and the lack of similar limitations of the income from capital would naturally tend to bring about a condition of inequality. But there is still another element of the situation to be taken into account.

Private property in the means of production implies for everyone the possibility of coming into possession of them, but it implies also the possibility of losing possession. That is, the craftsman may fall into absolute poverty. The existence of interest-bearing capital implies the existence of want. One who has what he needs will not borrow. By exploiting want, capital constantly increases it.

Here we have, then, the beginnings of modern conditions. Some "make" money without producing; others produce and remain in poverty. It is true that the evils of the system are not yet quite clear. The capitalist is dependent on the prosperity of the farmer and craftsman; his interest does not lie in dispossessing them entirely. Whole classes are not driven into poverty. Therefore poverty is regarded as a visitation of Providence, or as the result of shiftlessness or carelessness.

This way of looking at things is still common among the small capitalist class, and representatives of the present system, editors, lecturers, etc., strive to maintain popular faith in it. Private property in the means of production was once necessary to the good of society; there was a time when the average man had a chance to own property. This condition of affairs, they would have us believe, still exists. But in reality the nature of private property has changed. The old conditions have passed away absolutely. How this came about we are now to see.

3. The Capitalist Method of Production.

In the course of the Middle Ages the handicrafts developed steadily. There was a great increase in the division of labor—e. g., weaving divided into woolen weaving, linen weaving, etc. There was also increase in skill and improvement in tools. Simultaneouly there came about a development of trade, especially as a result of improved means of transportation by water.

Four hundred years ago the handicrafts were at their height. This was an eventful time in the history of commerce. The waterway to India came into use and America was discovered, with its endless supplies of gold and silver. A flood of wealth inundated Europe, wealth which the European adventurers had scooped up by means of barter, deceit and robbery. The lion's share of this wealth fell to the tradesmen able to fit out ships with bold, unscrupulous crews.

At the same time there came into being the modern state, the centralized official and military state, at first an absolute monarchy. This state met the demands of the rising capitalist class and depended on it for support. The modern state, the state of developed commodity-production, draws its power, not from personal service, but from its financial income. The monarchs had, therefore, every reason to protect and favor the capitalists who brought money into the country. In return the capitalists lent money to the monarchs, made debtors of them and put them in the position of dependents. This enabled them more and more to force the political and military power into their service. The state was obliged to improve means of communication, take over colonies and carry on wars in the interest of capital.

Our text-books on economics tell us that the beginning of capital is to be found in thrift. But we have learned that its origin was an altogether different one. Colonial policies were the chief sources of wealth open to capitalist nations; i. e., capital was drawn from plundering of foreign lands, from piracy, smuggling, slave-trading and war. Even down into the nineteenth century history shows us plenty of examples of this "thrift." And "thrifty" trades-people found in the state itself a powerful ally in this sort of "saving."

But newly discovered lands and commercial routes did more than bring wealth to the merchants; they opened up a new market for the seagoing nations of Europe, especially England. Handicraft was unable to satisfy the rapidly increasing demands of this market. These demands were on a large scale; production had to proceed on a large scale. That is, the market demanded a form of production which could and would adapt itself to the demand; in other words, a form absolutely in command of the merchants.

The merchants naturally found it to their interest to satisfy the demand of this new market; and they had the money to purchase the necessary means, raw materials, tools, factories and labor. But where was this last to come from? So long as a man owns tools of his own and can produce with them, he will not sell himself to another. Fortunately for the merchant, rural laborers were being driven from the soil. The landlords wanted their share of the new prosperity, therefore they enlarged their scale of production and demanded a larger proportion of the product. So agricultural laborers were forced to the doors of the new-built factories.

Thus the foundations of capitalist industry were laid by means of expropriation, by means of a revolution as bloody as any in history.

The separation of great masses of workers from the means of production, their transformation into propertyless proletarians, was a condition necessary to capitalist production. Economic development made the change inevitable. But the rising classes were not content to sit by and watch the course of events; they resorted to violence to accelerate the change. It was through violence of the most brutal, repulsive kind that capitalist society was ushered in.

4. The Death-Struggle of Small Production.

At first the new system differed but little from the old so far as external appearance was concerned. The capitalist delivered raw material to his hired workers and collected from them the finished product. Later he found it advantageous to gather them in a large building called a factory.

As soon as workers produced together in a factory, it was discovered that a division of labor increased the profits. Gradually systems of production became so developed that each operative had to make but a single motion or perform a single operation. That is, the laborer had been reduced to the level of a machine. Only one step remained—to replace him with a machine, and that step was soon taken. It was made possible by the development of science—and especially by the application of steam-power to industrial processes. The introduction of machinery meant an industrial revolution. With this change economic development became the triumphant march of capitalism.

Between 1770 and 1789 the first practical machines were introduced into the English textile industry. The steam engine was invented at the same time. From that period on the machine conquered one branch of industry after another and one country after another. It has placed it in the power of a factory operative to do the work of several hundred handicraftsmen.

Under these conditions the factory rules, and the days of handicraft, of independent production, are numbered. What remains is carried on chiefly by unfortunates who cannot find places in the factory system.

II. THE PROLETARIAT.

1. From Apprentice to Proletarian.

We have seen that the capitalist system of production implies the separation of the laborer from the means of production. On the one side there is the capitalist, who owns the machine, and on the other the proletarian, who does the work.

Originally it took forcible methods to secure the supply of proletarians necessary to this system. Today, however, such methods are no longer necessary. The economic power of the system has become sufficient to accomplish the desired result without breaking the law of private property. In fact, it is by the operation of this law that every year a sufficient number of farmers and independent craftsmen are given the choice between starvation and work in the factories.

That the number of the proletariat is steadily on the increase is such a palpable fact that no one attempts to deny it, not even those who would make us believe that society today rests on the same basis as it did a hundred years ago, and who try to paint the picture of the small producer in rosy colors. Indeed a change has taken place in the make-up of society, just as it has in the system of production. The capitalist form of production has overthrown all others, and become the dominant one in the field of industry; similarly wage-labor is today the dominant form of labor. A hundred years ago the farming peasantry took the first place; later, the small city industrialists; today it is the wage-earner.

In all civilized countries the proletarians are today the largest class; it is their condition and modes of thought that tend to control those of all the other divisions of labor. This implies a complete revolution in the condition and thought of the bulk of the population. The conditions of the proletariat differ radically from those of all former categories of labor. The small farmer, the artisan, the small producers generally, were the owners of the product of their labor by reason of their ownership of the means of production. The product of the labor of the proletarian does not belong to him, it belongs to the capitalist, to the owner of the requisite instruments of production. True enough, the proletarian is paid by the capitalist, but the value of his wages is far below that of his product.

When the capitalist in industry purchases the only commodity which the proletarian can offer for sale, that is, his labor-power, he does so for the sole purpose of utilizing it in a profitable way. The more the working-man produces, the larger the value of his product. If the capitalist were to work his employes only long enough to produce the worth of the wages he pays them, he would clear no profits. But his capital cries for profits and finds in him a willing listener. The longer the time is extended during which the workmen labor in the service of the capitalists, over and above the time needed to cover their wages, the larger is the value of their product, the larger is the surplus over and above the capitalist outlay in wages, and the larger is the per cent of exploitation to which these workmen are subjected. This exploitation of labor finds a limit only in the powers of endurance of the working people and in the resistance they may be able to offer to their exploiters.

In capitalist production, the capitalist and the wage-earner are not fellow-workers, as were the employer and employed in previous industrial epochs. The capitalist soon develops into, and remains, essentially a merchant. His activity, in so far as he is at all active, limits itself, like that of the merchant, to the operations of the market. His labors consist in purchasing as cheaply as possible the raw material, labor power and other essentials, and selling the finished products as dearly as possible. Upon the field of production itself he does nothing except to secure the largest quantity of labor from the workmen for the least possible amount of wages, and thereby to squeeze out of them the largest possible quantity of surplus values. In his relation to his employes he is not a fellow-worker, he is only a driver and exploiter. The longer they work, the better off he is; he is not tired out if the hours of labor are unduly extended; he does not perish if the method of production becomes a murderous one. The capitalist is vastly more reckless of the life and safety of his operatives than the master-workman of former times. Extension of the hours of labor, abolition of holidays, introduction of night labor, damp and overheated factories filled with poisonous gases, such are the "improvements" which the capitalist mode of production has introduced for the benefit of the working-class.

The introduction of machinery increases still further the danger to life and limb for the working-man. The machine system fetters him to a monster that moves perpetually with a gigantic power and with insane speed. Only the closest, never-flagging attention can protect the working-man attached to such a machine from being seized and broken by it. Protective devices cost money; the capitalist does not introduce them unless he is forced to do it. Economy being the much vaunted virtue of the capitalist, he is constrained by it to save room and to squeeze as much machinery as possible into the workshop. What cares he that the limbs of his working-men are thereby endangered? Working-men are cheap, but large, airy workshops are dear.

There is still another respect in which the capitalist employment of machinery lowers the condition of the working-class. It is this: the tool of the mechanic of former times was cheap and it was subject to few changes that would render it useless. It is otherwise with the machine; in the first place, it costs money, much money; in the second place, if through improvements in the system it becomes useless, or if it is not used to its full capacity, it will bring loss instead of profit to the capitalist. Again, the machine is worn out, not only through use, but through idleness. Furthermore, the introduction of science into production constantly causes new discoveries and inventions to take the place of the old ones. So, because they cannot compete with the improved machinery, now this machine, now that, and often whole factories at once, are rendered useless before they have been used to their full extent. Therefore, every machine is in danger of being made useless before it is used up; this is sufficient ground for the capitalist to utilize his machine as quickly as possible from the moment he puts it in operation. In other words, the capitalist application of the system of machinery is a spur that drives the capitalist to extend the hours of labor as much as possible, to carry on production without interruption, to introduce the system of night and day shifts, and, accordingly, to make of the unwholesome night work a permanent system.

At the time the system of machinery began to develop, some idealists declared the golden age was at hand; the machine was to release the working-man and render him free. In the hands of the capitalist, however, the machine has made the burden of labor unbearable.

But in the matter of wages, also, the condition of the wage-earner is worse than that of the medieval apprentice. The proletarian, the workman of today, does not eat at the table of the capitalist; he does not live in the same house. However wretched his home may be, however miserable his food, nay, even though he famish, the well-being of the capitalist is not disturbed by the sickening sight. The words wages and starvation used to be mutually exclusive; the free working-man formerly could starve only when he had no work. Whoever worked earned wages, he had enough to eat, starvation was not his lot.

For the capitalist system was reserved the un-
enviable distinction of reconciling these two op-
posites—wages and starvation—raising starva-
tion-wages into a permanent institution, even into
a prop of the present social system.

2. Wages.

Wages can never rise so high as to make it impossible for the capitalist to carry on his business
and to live from the profits of it; under such
circumstances it would be more profitable for the
capitalist to give up his business. Consequently,
the wages of the working-man can never rise
high enough to equal the value of his product.
They must always be below that, so as to leave a
surplus; it is only the prospect of a surplus that
moves the capitalist to purchase labor power. It
is therefore evident that under the capitalist system the wages of the workmen can never rise
high enough to put an end to the exploitation of
labor.

The surplus which the capitalist class appropriates is larger than is usually imagined. It covers not only the profits of the manufacturer, but
many other items that are usually credited to the
cost of production and exchange. It covers, for
instance, rent, interest on loans, salaries, merchant's profits, taxes, etc. All these have to be
subtracted from the surplus, that is, the excess
of the value of the product over the wages of the
working-man. It is evident that this surplus must
be a considerable one if a concern is to "pay."
It is clear that the wages of the working-man
cannot rise high enough to be even approximately

equal to the value of his profit. The capitalist system means under all circumstances the exploitation of the wage-workers. It is impossible to abolish this exploitation without abolishing the system itself. And the exploitation must be great even where wages are high.

But wages rarely reach the highest point which even these circumstances would permit; more often they are found to be nearer to the lowest possible point. This point is reached when the wages do not supply the workman with even the barest necessities. When the workman not only starves, but starves rapidly, all work is at an end.

The wages swing between these two extremes. The less the necessities of the workman, the larger the supply of labor on the market, and the slighter the capacity of the working-man for resistance, the lower wages sink.

In general, wages must be high enough to keep the working-man in a condition to work, or, to speak more accurately, they must be high enough to secure to the capitalist the measure of labor-power which he needs. In other words, wages must be high enough, not only to keep the working-men in a condition to work, but also in a condition to produce children to replace them.

Now industrial development exhibits a tendency, most pleasing to the capitalist, to lower the necessities of the working-man and to decrease his wages in proportion.

There was a time when skill and strength were requisites for a working-man. The period of apprenticeship was long, the cost of training con-

siderable. Now, however, the progress made in
the division of labor and the introduction of machinery render skill and strength in production
more and more superfluous; they make it possible to substitute unskilled and cheap workmen
for skilled ones; and, consequently, to put weak
women and even children in the place of men.
In the early stages of manufacturing this tendency is already perceptible; but not until machinery is introduced into production do we find
the wholesale exploitation of women and children—the most helpless among the helpless.

Originally, the wage-earner had to earn wages
high enough to defray, not only his own ex-
penses, but also those of his family, in order to
enable him to propagate himself and to bequeath
his labor power to others. Without this process
the heirs of the capitalists would find no proletarians ready made for exploitation.

When, however, the wife and young children
of the working-man are able to take care of
themselves, the wages of the male worker can
safely be reduced to the level of his own personal
needs without the risk of stopping the fresh supply of labor power.

The labor of women and children, moreover,
affords the additional advantage that these are
less capable of resistance than men; and their introduction into the ranks of the workers increases
tremendously the quantity of labor that is offered
for sale in the market.

Accordingly, the labor of women and children
not only lowers the necessities of the working-
man, it also diminishes his capacity for resist-

ance in that it overstocks the market; owing to both these circumstances it lowers the wages of the working-man.

3. Dissolution of the Proletarian Family.

The participation of women in industrial pursuits means the total destruction of the family life of the working-man without substituting for it a higher form of the family relation. The capitalist system of production does not in most cases destroy the single household of the working-man, but robs it of all but its unpleasant features. The activity of woman today in industrial pursuits does not mean to her freedom from household duties; it means an increase of her former burdens by a new one. But one cannot serve two masters. The household of the working-man suffers whenever his wife must help to earn the daily bread. Present society offers, in the place of the individual household which it destroys, only miserable substitutes; soup-houses and day-nurseries, where crumbs of the physical and mental sustenance of the rich are cast to the lower classes.

Socialists are charged with an intent to abolish the family. We do know that every system of production has had a special form of household to which corresponds a special system of family relationship. We do not consider the existing form of the family the highest possible, and we do expect that a new and improved social system will develop a new and higher form of family relationship. But to hold this view is a very different thing from trying to dissolve all family bonds. Those who do destroy the family bonds —who not only mean to, but actually do destroy them right under our eyes—are not the Socialists, but the capitalists. Many a slave-holder has in former times torn husband from wife and parents from children, but the capitalists have improved upon the abominations of slavery; they tear the infant from the breast of its mother and compel her to entrust it to strangers' hands. And yet a society in which hundreds of thousands of such instances are a daily occurrence, a society whose upper classes promote "benevolent" institutions for the purpose of making easy the separation of the mothers from their babies, such a society has the effrontery to accuse the Socialists of trying to abolish the family, because they, basing their opinion on the fact that the family has ever been one of the reflexes of the system of production, foresee that further changes in that system must also result in a more perfect family relationship.

4. Prostitution.

Hand in hand with the accusation on the subject of family bonds goes the charge that Socialists aim at a community of wives. This charge is as false as the other. Socialists, on the contrary, maintain that ideal love, just the reverse of a community of wives and of all sexual oppression and license, will be the foundation of matrimonial connections in a Socialist Commonwealth, and that pure love can prevail only in such a social system. What, on the other hand, do we see today?

Helpless women, forced to earn their living in factories, shops and mines, fall a prey to capitalist cupidity. The capitalist takes advantage of their inexperience, offers them wages too slight for their support, and hints at, or even brazenly suggests, prostitution as a means of supplementing their income. Everywhere the increase of female labor in industry is accompanied by an increase in prostitution. In the modern state where Christianity is so devoutedly preached, many a thriving branch of industry is found where working-women are paid so poorly that they would be compelled to starve did they not prostitute themselves. And the capitalists declare that the ability to compete, the prosperity of their industry, depend upon these low wages. Higher wages would ruin them.

Prostitution is as old as the contrast between rich and poor. At one time, however, prostitutes were a middle class between beggars and thieves; they were then an article of luxury in which society indulged but the loss of which would in no way have endangered its existence. To-day, however, it is no longer the females of the slums, alone, but working-women, who are compelled to sell their bodies for money. This latter sale is no longer simply a matter of luxury; it has become one of the foundations upon which production is carried on. Under the capitalist system prostitution becomes a pillar of society. What the defenders of this social system falsely charge Socialists with is the very thing they are guilty of themselves. Community of wives is a feature of capitalism. Indeed, such a deep root has this system of community of wives taken in modern society that its representatives agree in declaring prostitution to be a necessary thing. They cannot understand that the abolition of the proletariat implies the abolition of prostitution. So deep are they sunk in intellectual stagnation that they cannot conceive a social system without community of wives.

Community of wives is an invention of the upper classes of society, never of the proletariat. The community of wives is one of the modes of exploiting the proletariat; it is not Socialism, it is the exact opposite of Socialism.

5. The Industrial Reserve Army.

We have seen that the introduction of female and child-labor in industry is one of the most powerful means whereby the capitalists reduce the wages of working-men. There is, however, another means which, periodically, is just as powerful. This is the introduction of working-men from regions that are backward and whose population has slight wants, but whose labor-power has not yet been sapped by the factory system. The development of machinery makes possible, not only the employment of such untrained working-men in the place of trained ones, but also their cheap and prompt transportation to the place where they are wanted. Hand in hand with the development of production goes the system of transportation; colossal production corresponds to colossal transportation, not only of merchandise, but also of persons. Steamships and railroads, these much-vaunted pillars of civilization, not only carry guns, liquor and syphilis to barbarians, they also bring the barbarians and their barbarism to us. The flow of agricultural laborers into the cities is becoming constantly stronger; and from ever farther regions are the swarms of those drawing near who have fewer wants, are more patient and offer less resistance. There is a constant stream of emigration from one country of Europe to another, from Europe to America and even from the Orient to western lands. These foreign workers are partly expropriated people, small farmers and producers, whom the capitalist system of production has ruined, driven on the street and deprived not only of a home, but also of a country. Look at these numberless emigrants and ask whether it is Socialism which robs them of their country.

Through the expropriation of the small producers, through the importation from distant lands of large masses of labor, through the use of the labor of women and children, through the shortening of the time necessary to acquire a trade,—through all these means the capitalist system of production is able to increase stupendously the quantity of labor forces at its disposal. And side by side with this goes a steady increase in the productivity of human labor as a result of the uninterrupted progress in the technical arts.

Simultaneously with these tendencies the machine tends steadily to displace workmen and render them superfluous. Every machine saves labor-power; unless it did that, it would be useless. In every branch of industry the transition from hand to machine labor is accompanied by

the greatest suffering to the working-men who are
affected by it. Whether they are factory workers
or independent craftsmen, they are made superfluous by the machine and thrown out upon the
streets. It was this effect of machinery that the
workingmen felt first. Many riots during the
first year of the nineteenth century attest the suffering which the transition from hand to machine
labor, or the introduction of new machinery, in-
flicts upon the working-class and the despair to
which they are driven thereby. The introduction
of machinery, as well as its subsequent improvement, is always harmful to certain divisions of
labor. True enough, under some conditions other
working-men, for instance, those who make the
machines, may profit by it. But it may be
doubted whether a consciousness of this fact affords much comfort to those who are starving.

Every new machine causes as much to be produced as before by fewer workmen, or larger
production with no increase in the number of
workmen. From this it follows that, if the number of workmen employed in a country does not
decrease with the development of the system of
machinery, the market must be extended in proportion to the increased productivity of these
workers. But since the economic development increases the productivity of labor at the same time
that it increases the quantity of disposable labor,
it follows that, in order to prevent enforced idleness among workmen, the market must be extended at a much more rapid pace than that at
which the productivity of labor is increased by
the machine. Such a rapid extension of the mar-

ket has, however, rarely occurred under the rule of capitalist production. Therefore, enforced idleness is a permanent phenomenon under the capitalist system of production, and is inseparable from it. Even in the best times when the market suddenly undergoes a considerable extension and business is brisk, production is not able to furnish work for all the unemployed. During bad times, however, when business is at a standstill, their number reaches enormous proportions. They constitute, with the workers of superfluous small concerns, a great army, "the industrial reserve army," as Marx called it, an army of labor forces that stands ever ready at the disposal of the capitalist, an army out of which he can draw his reserves whenever the industrial campaign grows hot.

To the capitalist this reserve army is invaluable. It places in his hands a powerful weapon with which to curb the army of the employed. After excessive work on the part of some has produced lack of work for others, then the idleness of these is used as a means to keep up, and even increase, the excessive work of the former. And yet there are people who will contend that matters are today arranged in the best possible way!

Although the size of the industrial reserve army rises and falls with the ups and downs of business, nevertheless, on the whole it shows a steady tendency to increase. This is inevitable. The technical development moves on at a constantly increasing pace and steadily extends its field of operations, while, on the other hand, the extension of the markets is hemmed in by natural limits.

What, then, is the full significance of lack of work? It signifies not only want and misery to the unemployed, not only intensified servitude and exploitation to the employed; it signifies also uncertainty of livelihood for the whole working class. Whatever hardships former modes of exploitation inflicted upon the exploited, one boon was left them: the certainty of a livelihood. The sustenance of the serf and the slave was assured at least during the life of the master himself. Only when the master perished was the life of his dependents in peril. Whatever amount of misery and want afflicted the people under former systems of production, it never resulted from production itself; it was the result of a disturbance of production, brought on by failure of crops, drouths, floods, invasions of hostile armies, etc.

Today the existence of the exploiter is not bound up in that of the exploited. At any moment the workman, with his wife and children, can be thrown upon the street and given over to starvation without the exploiter, whom he has made rich, being the worse for it.

The misery of enforced idleness is today rarely the result of a disturbance in production caused by outside influences; it is the necessary result of the development of the present system of production. Just the reverse happens of what occurred under the former systems of production; disturbances of production often improve the opportunities for work rather than lessening them; remember the results of the war of 1870 upon the industrial life of Germany and France in the years immediately following.

Under our former system of production on a small scale the income of the worker was in proportion to his industry. Laziness ruined him and finally threw him out of work. Today, on the contrary, unemployment becomes greater the harder and the longer the workman toils; he brings enforced idleness upon himself through his own labor. Among the many maxims from the world of small production which capitalist large production has reversed is: "A man's industry is his fortune."

Labor-power is no more a shield against want and misery than is property. As the specter of bankruptcy hovers always over the small farmer and the craftsman, so the specter of unemployment hovers always over the wage-earner. Of all the ills which attend the present system of production the most trying, that which harrows men's souls deepest and pulls up by the roots every instinct of conservatism, is the permanent uncertainty of a livelihood. This constant uncertainty as to one's own condition undermines one's belief in the permanence of the existing order and one's interest in its preservation. Whoever is kept in eternal fear by the existing order loses all fear of a new one.

Excessive work, lack of work, the destruction of the family—these are the gifts that the capitalist system of production brings to the proletariat, and at the same time it forces more and more of the population into proletarian conditions of living.

6. The Increase of the Proletariat. Mercantile and Educated Proletariat.

It is not only through the extension of large production that the capitalist system causes the condition of the proletariat to become more and more that of the whole population. It brings this about also through the fact that the condition of the wage-earner engaged in large production strikes the keynote for the condition of the wage-earners in all other branches. The conditions under which the latter work and live are revolutionized; the advantages which they may have had over those engaged in capitalist industry are turned into so many disadvantages under the influence of the latter. To illustrate: Where, for example, the craftsman still boards and lives with his master, this arrangement becomes a means of forcing him to be content with even poorer board and lodging than those of the wage-earner who carries on his own household.

There is another and very extensive domain in which the capitalist system of large production tends to turn the population into proletarians— the domain of commerce. The large stores are already bearing heavily upon the smaller ones. The number of small stores does not, for that reason, diminish. On the contrary, it increases. The small store is the last refuge of the bankrupt small producer. Were the small stores actually crowded out, the ground would be wholly taken from under the feet of the small traders; they would then be thrust forthwith below the class of the proletariat—into the slums; they would be turned into beggars, vagabonds and candidates for the penitentiary—a wonderful social reform!

But it is not in the reduction of the number of small stores, it is in the debasement of their character that the influence of large production manifests itself in commerce. The small trader deals in ever worse and cheaper goods; his life becomes more precarious, more proletarian. In the large stores, on the contrary, there is constant increase in the number of employes—genuine proletarians without prospect of ever becoming independent. Child labor, the labor of women, with its accompaniment of prostitution, excessive work, lack of work, starvation wages—all the symptoms of large production—appear also in increasing quantity in the domain of commerce. Steadily the condition of the employes in this department approaches that of the proletarians in the department of production. The only difference perceptible between the two is that the former preserve the appearances of a better living, which require sacrifices unknown to the industrial proletarians.

There is still a third category of proletarians that has gone far on the road to its complete development—the educated proletarians. Education has become a special trade under our present system. The measure of knowledge has increased greatly and grows daily. Capitalist society and the capitalist state are increasingly in need of men of knowledge and ability to conduct their business, in order to bring the forces of nature under their power. But not only the hard-working small farmer, mechanic or the proletarian in general have no time to devote themselves to science and art; the merchant, the manufacturer, the banker, the stock-jobber, the landlord—all are in the same situation. Their whole time is taken up with their business and their pleasures. In modern society it is not, as it used to be under previous social orders, the exploiters themselves, or at least a class of them, who foster the arts and sciences. The present exploiters, our ruling class, leave these pursuits to a special class whom they keep in hire. Under this system education becomes a merchandise.

A hundred years or so ago this commodity was rare. There were few schools; study was accompanied with considerable expense. So long as small production could support him, the worker stuck to it; only special gifts of nature or favorable circumstances would cause the sons of the workers to dedicate themselves to the arts and sciences. Though there was an increasing demand for teachers, artists and other professional men, the supply was definitely limited.

So long as this condition of things lasted, education commanded a high price. Its possession produced, at least for those who applied it to practical ends, very comfortable livings; not infrequently it brought honor and fame. The artist, the poet, the philosopher, were, in monarchical countries, the companions of royalty. The aristocracy of intellect felt itself superior to the aristocracy of birth or money. The only care of such was the development of their intellect. Hence it happened that people of culture could be, and often were, idealists. These aristocrats of education and culture stood above the other

classes and their material aspirations and antagonisms. Education meant power, happiness and
worth. The conclusion seemed inevitable that in
order to make all men happy and worthy, in
order to banish all class antagonisms, all poverty,
all wickedness and meanness out of the world,
nothing else was needed than to spread education
and culture.

Since those days the development of higher education has made immense progress. The number of institutions of learning has increased wonderfully, and in a still larger degree, the number
of pupils. In the meantime the bottom has
been knocked out of small production. The small
property holder knows today no other way of
keeping his sons from sinking into the proletariat
than sending them to college; and he does this
if his means will at all allow. But, furthermore,
he must consider the future not only of his sons,
but also of his daughters. The development in
the division of labor is rapidly encroaching on
the household; it is converting one household
duty after another into a special industry, and
steadily diminishing household work. Weaving,
sewing, knitting, baking, and many other occupations that at one time filled up the round of
household duties, have been either wholly or partially withdrawn from the sphere of housekeep-
ing. As a result of all this, marriage in which
the wife is to be the housekeepr only, is becoming more and more a matter of luxury. But it
so happens that the small property holder and
producer is at the same time sinking steadily, and
steadily becoming poorer; more and more he

loses the means to indulge in luxury. In consequence of this the number of unmarried women increases, and ever larger is the number of those families in which mother and daughter must become wage-earners. Accordingly the number of women wage-earners increases, not only in large and small production and commerce, but in government offices, in the telegraph and telephone service, in railroads and banks, in the arts and sciences. However loudly personal interests and prejudices may rebel against it, the labor of women presses itself forward more and more into the various professional pursuits. It is not vanity, nor forwardness nor arrogance, but the force of economic development that drives women to labor in these as well as in other fields of human activity. If men have succeeded in preventing the competition of women in certain branches of intellectual labor which are still organized on craft lines, women workers tend to crowd all the more into the pursuits not so organized, for example, authorship, painting, music.

The result of this whole development is that the number of educated people has increased enormously. Nevertheless, the beneficent results which the idealists expected from an increase of education have not followed. So long as education is a merchandise, its extension is equivalent to an increase in the quantity of that merchandise, consequently to the falling in its price and the decline in the condition of those who possess it. The number of educated people has grown to such an extent that it more than suffices for the

wants of the capitalists and the capitalist state.
The labor market of educated labor is today as
overstocked as the market of manual labor. It
is no longer the manual workers alone who have
their reserve army of the unemployed and are afflicted with lack of work; the educated workers
also have their reserve army of idle, and among
them also lack of work has taken up its permanent quarters. The seekers for public office find
that avenue of employment crowded. Those who
seek openings elsewhere experience the extremes
of idleness and excessive work just as do the
manual workers, and like them are the victims of
wage-slavery.

The condition of the educated workers deteri-
orates visibly; formerly people spoke of the "aristocracy of intellect," today we speak of the "intellectual" or "educated" proletariat.

The time is near when the bulk of these proletarians will be distinguished from the others only
by their pretensions. Most of them still imagine
that they are something better than proletarians.
They fancy they belong to the bourgeoisie, just
as the lackey identifies himself with the class of
of his master. They have ceased to be the leaders of the capitalist class and have become rather
their defenders. Place-hunting takes more and
more of their energies. Their first care is, not
the development of their intellect, but the sale of
it. The prostitution of their individuality has become their chief means of advancement. Like
the small producers, they are dazzled by the few
brilliant prizes in the lottery of life; they shut
their eyes to the numberless blanks in the wheel
and barter away soul and body for the merest

chance of drawing such a prize. The barter and sale of one's convictions and the marriage for money are, in the eyes of most of our educated proletarians, two means, as natural as they are necessary, to "make one's fortune."

Still, the supply of this class grows so rapidly that there is little to be made out of education, even though one throws his individuality into the bargain. The decline of the mass of educated people into the class of the proletariat can no longer be checked.

Whether this development will result in a movement of the educated people to join the battling proletariat in mass and not, as hitherto, singly, is still uncertain. This however, is certain: The fact that the educated people are being forced into the proletariat has closed to the proletarians the only gate through which its members could, by dint of their own unaided efforts, escape into the class above.

The possibility of the wage-earner becoming a capitalist is, in the ordinary run of events, out of the question. Sensible people do not consider the chance of winning a prize in a lottery or of falling heir to the wealth of some unknown relative when they deal with the condition of the working-class. Under certain particularly favorable conditions it has sometimes happened that a workman succeeded, through great privations, in saving up enough to start a little industry of his own, or to set up a little retail shop, or to give his son a chance to study and become something "better" than his father. But it was always ridiculous to hold out such possibilities to the workman as a means of improving his condition. In the ordinary course of events the working-man may thank his stars if he is at all able, even during good times, to lay by enough not to remain empty-handed when work becomes slack. Today, however, to hold out such hopes to working-men is more ridiculous than ever.* The economic development makes saving not only more difficult, but it renders it impossible for a working-man, even if he succeeds in saving something, to pull himself and his children out of the class of the proletariat. To invest his little savings in some small independent industry were for him to fall from the frying pan into the fire; ten to one he will be thrown back to his previous condition, with the bitter experience that the small producer can no longer keep his head above water—an experience which he will have purchased with the loss of his hard-earned savings.

Today, whichever way the proletarian may turn, he finds awaiting him the same proletarian conditions of life. These conditions pervade society more and more. In all countries the mass of the population has sunk to the level of the proletariat. To the individual proletarian the prospect has vanished of ever being able, by his own efforts, to pull himself out of the quagmire into which the present system of production has pushed him. The individual proletarian can accomplish his own redemption only with the redemption of his whole class.

---

*Note.—In America the conditions under which a proletarian is able to rise into the bourgeois class have been prolonged by the abundance of our natural resources and the existence of an open frontier. But if the author's statements in regard to this matter are not strictly applicable to our society, they tend more and more to become so.—Translator.

III. THE CAPITALIST CLASS.

1. Commerce and Credit.

In countries where the capitalist system of production prevails the masses of the people are forced down to the condition of proletarians; that is to say, of workers who are divorced from their instruments of production so that they can produce nothing by their own efforts, and, therefore, are compelled to sell the only commodity they possess—their labor-power. To this class, also, belong the majority of the farmers, small producers and traders; the little property they still possess today is but a thin veil, calculated rather to conceal than to prevent their dependence and exploitation.

Over against this class we find a small group of property holders—capitalists and landlords—who alone possess the most important means of production and the most important sources of livelihood, the exclusive ownership of which invests them with the power to subjugate the class of propertyless and to exploit them.

While the majority of the people sink ever deeper in want and misery, this small group of capitalists and landlords, together with their parasites, appropriate all the tremendous advantages that have been wrung from nature, especially through the progress made by the natural sciences and their practical application.

There are three sorts of capital: merchant's capital, interest-bearing capital and industrial capital. The last of these is the youngest; perhaps it is not as many hundred years old as the other two are thousands. But the youngest of these brothers has grown faster, much faster, than either of his seniors; he has become a giant who has enslaved and forced them into his service.

In its classic form small production was not dependent on commerce. The farmer and the mechanic could acquire the means of production, in so far as they needed any, direct from the producer; furthermore, they could sell their product directly to the consumer. Commerce, at that stage of economic development, catered chiefly to luxury; it was not then a matter of necessity, either for the promotion of production or for the support of society.

Capitalist production, however, is from the very start dependent upon commerce; and *vice versa,* from a certain stage on, commerce needs capitalist production for its further development. The further the capitalist system of production extends, and the more dominant it becomes, the more requisite is the development of commerce to the whole industrial life. Commerce today no longer caters simply to superfluity and luxury. The whole system of production, yes, even the sustenance of the people, in a capitalist country, depends now upon the free and unrestricted action of commerce. This is one of the reasons why war is more devastating than ever; it interrupts commerce, and that has become equivalent to a stoppage of production, to a suspension of economic life, and to an industrial ruin that spreads beyond the field of battle and is not less mischievous than the devastation that takes place there.

As important as the development of commerce is that of interest to the capitalist system of production. In the days of the small producer the money-lender was simply a parasite, who profited by the distress or improvidence of others. The money which he lent to others was, as a rule, put to unproductive uses. If, for instance, a nobleman borrowed money, he did so to spend it in pleasure; if a farmer or mechanic borrowed money, it was mainly to pay his taxes or the cost of lawsuits. In those days lending at interest was considered immoral and was everywhere condemned.

Under the capitalist system of production this has all changed. Money is now a means whereby to establish a capitalist industry, to buy and to exploit labor-power. When today a capitalist raises money in order to establish a factory, or to enlarge one already in existence it does not follow—provided, of course, that his undertaking prosper—that his previous income will be reduced by the interest on the loan. The loan, on the contrary, helps him to exploit labor-power, consequently, to increase his income by an amount larger than the interest he will have to pay. Therefore, under the capitalist system of production, lending has lost its original character. Its role as a means for the exploitation of distress or improvidence is pushed to the rear by a new one, that of "fructifying" the capitalist system of production, that is to say, of enabling it to develop faster than it otherwise would by the mere hoarding of capital in the vaults of industrial capitalists. The horror once entertained for a lender has come to an end; he now becomes a spotless character and receives a new and euphonious name, creditor.

Simultaneously with this metamorphosis, the principal current of interest-bearing capital underwent a change. The money which the lenders heaped up in their vaults flowed formerly out of those reservoirs, through a thousand channels, into the hands of the non-capitalists. Today, on the contrary, the vaults of the lenders, the institutions of credit, have become the reservoirs into which there flow, through a thousand channels, money from non-capitalists, and out of which this money is then conveyed to the capitalist. Credit is today, just as it was formerly, a means whereby to render non-capitalists—whether property holders or propertyless—subject to the payment of interest; today, however, it has, further, become a powerful instrument wherewith to convert into capital the property in the hands of the various classes of non-capitalists, from the large estates of endowed institutions and aristocrats down to the pennies saved by servant girls and day laborers. In other words, it has become an instrument for the displacing of the old propertied classes and the intensified exploitation of the wage-earners. People praise the present institutions of credit, savings banks, etc., thinking that they turn the small savings of working-men, servant girls and farmers into capital and these unfortunates themselves into "capitalists." Nevertheless, the only object in collecting the money of non-capitalists is to place at the disposal of capitalists an increased quantity of capital and thus to accelerate the development of the capitalist system of production. What this means to wage-earners, small farmers and mechanics we have already seen.

At the same time that the present institutions of credit are converting the whole property of non-capitalists into capital and placing it at the disposal of the capitalist class, they see to it that the capital of the capitalist class itself is better utilized than before. They become the reservoirs of all the money which the individual capitalist may, from time to time, have no occasion to use, and they make these sums, which otherwise would have lain "dead," accessible to such other capitalists as may stand in need of them. Furthermore, they make it possible to convert merchandise into money before it is sold, and thereby diminish the quantity of capital formerly needed in a given business undertaking.

Through all these means the quantity and power of the capital at the disposal of the capitalist class is enormously increased. Hence it is that credit has now become one of the most powerful levers of the capitalist system of production. Next to the great development of machinery and the creation of the reserve army of unemployed labor, credit is the principal cause of the rapid development of the present system.

Credit is, however, much more sensitive than commerce to any disturbance. Every shock it receives is felt throughout the economic organization.

Many political economists have looked upon credit as a means whereby people without any, or with little, property could be turned into capitalists. But, as its name indicates, credit rests upon the confidence of him who gives, in him who takes, credit. The more the latter possesses, the grater is the security that he offers, and the greater is the security that he enjoys. Consequently, credit is only a means whereby more money may be furnished to the capitalists than they possess, thereby to increase their preponderance and to draw sharper the social antagonisms, instead of to weaken or remove them.

To sum up, credit is not only a means whereby to develop the capitalist system of production more rapidly, and to enable it to turn to use every favorable opportunity; it is also a means whereby to promote the downfall of small production; and, lastly, it is a means to render modern industry more and more complicated and liable to disturbance, to carry the feeling of uncertainty into the ranks of the capitalists themselves and to make the ground upon which they move ever more uncertain.

2. Division of Labor and Competition.

While, on the one hand, the industrial development draws commerce and credit in ever closer relation with industry, it brings about, on the other hand, an increased division of labor; the various functions which the capitalist has to fulfill in the industrial life, divide more and more and fall to the part of separate undertakings and institutions. Formerly, it was the merchant's function not only to buy and sell goods, but to store them, and often to carry them to far distant markets. He had to assort his goods, display them, and render them accessible to the individual purchaser. Today there is a division of labor not between wholesale and retail trade only; we find also large undertakings for the transportation and the storing of goods. In those large central markets called exchanges, buying and selling have to such an extent become separate pursuits and freed themselves from the other functions commonly pertaining to the merchant, that not only are goods located in distant regions, or even not yet produced, bought and sold there, but that goods are bought without the purchaser intending to take possession of them, and others are sold without the seller ever having had them in his possession.

In former days a capitalist could not be conceived without the thought of a large safe into which money was collected and out of which he took the funds which he needed to make payments. Today the treasury of the capitalist has become the subject of a separate occupation in all industrially advanced countries, especially England and America. The bank has sprung up. Payments are no longer made to a capitalist, but to his bank, and from his bank, not from him, are his debts collected. And so it happens that a few central concerns perform today the functions of treasury for the whole capitalist class of the country.

But although the several functions of the capitalist thus become the functions of separate undertakings, they do not become independent of each other except in appearance and legal form; economically, they remain as closely bound to and dependent upon each other as ever. The functions of any of these undertakings could not continue if those of any of the others with which they are connected were to be interrupted.

The more commerce, credit and industry become interdependent and the more the separate functions of the capitalist class are assumed by separate undertakings, the greater is the dependence of one capitalist upon another. Capitalist production becomes, accordingly, more and more a gigantic body, whose various limbs are in the closest relation to each other. Thus, while the masses of the people become ever more dependent upon the capitalists, the capitalists themselves become ever more dependent upon one another.

The economic machinery of the modern system of production constitutes a more and more delicate and complicated mechanism; its uninterrupted operation depends constantly more upon whether each of its wheels fits in with the others and does the work expected of it. Never yet did any system of production stand in such need of careful direction as does the present one. But the institution of private property makes it impossible to introduce plan and order into this system.

While the several industries become, in point of fact, more and more dependent upon one another, in point of law, they remain wholly independent. The means of production in every sin-

gle industry are private property; their owner
can do with them as he pleases.

The farther large production develops, the
larger every single industry becomes, the better
is the order to which the economic activity of
each is reduced, and the more accurate and well-
considered is the plan upon which each is carried
on, down to the smallest details. The joint operation of the various industries is, however, left
to the blind force of free competition. It is at
the expense of a prodigious waste of power and
of materials and under stress of constantly increasing economic crises that free competition
keeps the industrial mechanism in motion. The
process goes on, not by putting every one in his
place, but by crushing everyone who stands in
the way. This is what is called "the survival of
the fittest in the struggle for existence." The fact
is, however, that competition crushes, not so much
the truly unfit, as those who happen to stand in
the wrong place, and who lack either the special
qualifications or, what is more important, the capital to survive. But competition is no longer satisfied with crushing those who are unequal to the
"struggle for existence." The destruction of
every one of these draws in its wake the ruin of
numberless others who were economically connected with the bankrupt concern—wage-earners, creditors, etc.

"Every man is the architect of his own fortune." So runs a favorite proverb. This proverb
is an heirloom from the days of small production,
when the fate of every single bread-winner, at
most that of his family also, depended upon his

own personal qualities. Today the fate of every member of a capitalist community depends less and less upon his own individuality, and more and more upon a thousand circumstances that are wholly beyond his control. Competition no longer brings about the survival of the fittest.

3. Profit.

Whence does the capitalist class derive its income? The gains of merchant's and lender's capital consisted originally of the portions which they withheld from the property of those dependent on them, who might represent any of the various classes. It is otherwise with industrial capital. It so happens that in proportion as the capitalist system of production develops, the industrial form of capital overshadows all others and forces them into its service. Furthermore, it can do this only in so far as it returns to them a part of the surplus value which it has drawn from the workers. As a result of this development the surplus produced by the proletarians becomes more and more the only source from which the whole capitalist class draws its income.

As the small industrialist and the small farmer are disappearing and their influence upon modern society is felt ever less, so also are disappearing the old forms of merchant's and interest-bearing capital, both of which made their gains by exploiting the non-capitalist classes. Already there are nations without independent artisans and small farmers. England is an instance in point. But no one can conceive of a single modern state without large production. Whoever desires to understand the modern forms of capital must proceed from the industrial form that capital has assumed. The real and increasingly important source from which flow capitalist gains is to be found in the surplus value produced by capital industry.

We have in the preceding chapter become acquainted with the surplus value which the industrial proletarian produces and the industrial capital appropriates. We have also seen how the amount of the surplus value produced by the individual laborer increases at a more rapid rate than does his wage; this is brought about by the increase in the amount of labor, introducing labor-saving machinery and cheaper forms of labor. At the same time there is an increase in the number of proletarians. So the amount of the surplus accruing to the capitalist class swells constantly more and more.

Unfortunately, however, "life's unalloyed enjoyment is not the lot of mortal man." However distasteful it may be to him, the capitalist is compelled to "divide" with the landowner and the state. And the share claimed by each of these increases from year to year.

4. Rent.

When one speaks of the classes which are steadily becoming the sole property holders and exploiters, the monopolists of the instruments of production, distinction must be made between the capitalists and landlords.

The land is a peculiar means of production. It is the most necessary of all; without it no human

activity is possible; even the sailor and the aero-
naut need a point of departure and a landing
place. Furthermore, it is a means of production
that cannot be increased at pleasure. For all this
it must be noted that as yet it has but rarely happened that every inch of ground in any state was
actually occupied or used productively by its in-
habitants; even in China there are still wide
stretches of unproductive land.

In medieval Europe each farmer possessed his
buildings and parcel of land. Water, forest and
pasture were municipal property, and there was
enough land so that each might be given possession of any which he reduced to cultivation.
Then came the development of commodity-pro
duction. The products of the land now had an
exchange value. As a result the land also became, as it were, a product; it had a value. As
soon as this occurred the communities began to
limit their numbers and take measures to insure
the perpetual possession of lands; they became
close corporations.

But another class, the feudal lords, were also
yearning for the communal property. And in
regions where farming on a large scale had developed they succeeded in driving the small farmers from the soil. In the course of events practically all land became the private property of a
few.

Thus a monopoly has come into existence, and
a monopoly of an altogether extraordinary sort.
The earth's surface is held by a few, not only
against the propertyless proletarian class, but
against part of the capitalist class itself. A part

of the industrial capitalist class may for a time monopolize a branch of industry, but its monopoly is never absolute or permanent. In these respects the land monopolists have the advantage, their monopoly may be both absolute and lasting.

This form of capitalism is most highly developed in England, where a small number of families have possession of all the land. Whoever needs land obtains the use of it only by paying rent. As a rule the capitalist cannot buy land for a factory or dwelling. Thus a part of his profit always goes to the landlord.

In most parts of the world, however, the line is not so sharply drawn. On the continent of Europe, for example, the capitalist manufacturer, mine operator, etc., usually owns the land necessary to his operations. The great landowners, on their part, usually carry on their farming operations themselves.

On the other hand, as capitalism develops, proletarians are more and more herded in cities. This leads to an unprecedented heightening of land values and a reinforcement of the position of the land-owning class. Workers must pay higher and higher rent, and this, in turn, necessitates an increase in their wages. Thus once more the industrial capitalist is forced to share his spoils with the land-owner.

5. Taxes.

If the landlord appropriates a constantly increasing proportion of the capitalist's surplus value, the state is not less active in the same direction. The modern state grew with and through the capitalist class, just as, in turn, it has become the most powerful support of this class. Each has promoted the interests of the other. The capitalist class cannot forego the assistance of the state. It needs the powerful hand of government to protect it against foes within and without.

The further the capitalist system of production develops, the sharper become the contrasts and contradictions which it brings forth, the more complex becomes its operation, the greater the dependence of individuals upon each other, and consequently the more imperative the need of an authority which will see to it that each fulfills his economic functions. A process so sensitive as modern production can endure less easily than any previous one the strain attendant on the settling of differences by individual trials of strength. In place of self-dependence appears now a legal system fostered by the state.

The capitalist system is by no means the product of political rights or laws. It is, on the contrary, the needs of the system that have brought forth the laws that are now in force. These laws do not create the exploitation of the proletariat; they only provide for the smooth running of the system of exploitation, together with all the other processes pertaining to the existing social order. Competition being styled the mainspring of production, law may be designated as a lubricating oil, the object of which is to diminish as much as possible the friction produced by the present social mechanism.

As the conditions which produce this friction

grow gradually worse, the greater becomes the need of a strong state power to enforce the law. For example, the constantly increasing opposition between exploiters and exploited, propertied and propertyless, steadily augments the slum element in our population and thus increases the necessity for a large police force. On the other hand, as each capitalist becomes more and more dependent on the co-operation of others of his class, the more he becomes dependent on the decrees of the courts.

But the capitalist is concerned not only with peaceful manufacture and trade within his own country. Foreign trade has from the beginning played an important part in our industrial system, and the greater the extent to which it becomes the controlling interest, the more does the securing and developing of foreign markets become one of the chief concerns of the entire nation. But in the world-market the capitalists of one nation meet those of another as competitors. In order to oppose these competitors, they call upon their government to maintain their rights, or, better yet, to drive out their foreign competitors altogether. Thus as states and monarchs become more and more dependent on the capitalist class armies and navies become more exclusively the tools of this class. Wars are no more dynastic, but commercial, and finally national; they result from economic competition between the capitalists of different nations.

Thus the capitalist system needs, not only an army of officials to operate courts and police departments, but also an army of soldiers. Both armies tend to grow rapidly, but during recent years the latter has oustripped the former. Furthermore, the application of modern science to warfare has enormously increased its cost. As a result, the military expenditures of the great world-states have increased incredibly.

The state is becoming constantly more expensive, its burdens ever heavier. Capitalists and landowners try everywhere to foist these burdens upon the other classes. But the poorer classes grow constantly less able to pay, and so despite their cunning, the exploiters are obliged to increase the share of profits which they turn over to the state.

6. The Falling Off in the Rate of Profit.

Simultaneously with this development, the quantity of the capital which the capitalist class applies productively shows a tendency to increase more rapidly than the exploitation of the working-class, that is to say, more rapidly than the mass of surplus which the latter creates.

To illustrate: Compare a spinner of a hundred years ago with a machine-weaver of today. How enormous is the capital required to enable the latter to work! On the other hand, the capital which the capitalist invested in hand-weaving was trifling in comparison. The exploited hand-spinner may have worked at home. In that case the capitalist paid him his wages and gave him the cotton or flax which he needed. In point of wages there has not been much change, but a machine-weaver consumes today in production a hundred times more raw material than the former hand-weaver; over and above that, how tremendous are today the buildings, power engines, looms, etc., necessary to carry on the industry.

There is still another thing to be considered. The only outlays of the capitalist who a hundred years ago employed a spinner were for wages and raw material, there was not then any fixed capital, for the cost of the spinning-wheel was too trifling to consider. He turned his capital over quickly, say every three months; as a result of this, he needed, to start with, only one-quarter of the capital which he used during the whole year. Today the capital invested in a spinning-mill for machinery and buildings is enormous. Even though the time within which the capitalist could get back the sum he pays out in wages and for raw materials were now the same as it was a hundred years ago, the time which it now takes him to get back the rest of his capital, which a hundred years ago he hardly needed, has become a very long one.

A number of circumstances work in the opposite direction. Among these the most important are the recently developed system of credit and the decline in the value of products, the latter of which is the inevitable result of the increase in the productivity of labor. But neither of these causes is sufficient to counteract the effect of the others. In all branches of production, in some slowly, in others rapidly, the quantity of capital necessary for production grows perceptibly from year to year.

Let it be assumed that the capital necessary for a certain industry a hundred years ago was $100, and that today the amount necessary is $1,000, and, furthermore, that the amount exploited from labor is now five times as large as then, *i. e.,* that whereas the surplus which labor formerly produced was $50, today it is $250. In this case the quantity of the surplus has increased absolutely; nevertheless, in proportion to the quantity of capital invested, the surplus value has decreased. A hundred years ago this proportion was 50 per cent, today it is only 25 per cent. This instance is simply an illustration meant to point out a tendency.

The total amount of surplus yearly produced in this, as a capitalist country, increases rapidly; but still more rapidly grows the total amount of capital invested by the capital class in their establishments. If now it be considered that taxation and rent carry off yearly an ever larger portion of the capitalists' surplus, the phenomenon may be explained that the quantity of surplus that will accrue to a certain amount of capital tends steadily to diminish, notwithstanding that the amount of exploitation of labor tends steadily to increase.

Accordingly, profit, that is to say, the portion of the surplus produced by labor which a capitalist retains, shows a tendency to decline in proportion to the quantity of capital he invests. Or, to put it another way, in the course of the development of the capitalist system of production, the profit which a given quantity of capital yields tends to go down. This, of course, holds good only on the average and during long periods of time. An evidence of this downward tendency of profit is the steady decline of interest.

It happens, therefore, that while the exploitation of the working-man tends to rise, the rate of capitalist profit has a tendency to sink. This fact is one of the most remarkable contradictions of the capitalist system of production—a system that bristles with contradictions.

Some there are who have concluded from this sinking of profits that the capitalist system of exploitation will put an end to itself, that capital will eventually yield so little profit that starvation will force the capitalists to look for work. This conclusion would be correct, if, as the rate of profits sank, the quantity of invested capital remained the same. This, however, is by no means the case. The total quantity of capital in all capitalist nations grows at a more rapid pace than the rate of profit declines. The increase of capital is a prerequisite to the sinking of profit, and if a capitalist's investment has increased from one million to two, and from two million to four, his income is not reduced when the rate of profit sinks from 5 per cent to 4, and from 4 to 3.

The decline of the rate of profit, and likewise of interest, in no way implies a reduction of the income of the capitalist class, for the mass of surplus that flows into its hands grows constantly larger; the decline diminishes solely the income of those capitalists who are not able correspondingly to increase their capital. In the course of industrial development, it takes a constantly increasing amount of capital to support its owner with the "dignity of his class." The quantity of capital requisite to free its owner from labor, and to enable him to live on the labor of others, becomes constantly larger. The sum which fifty years ago was a considerable fortune is today an insignificant pittance.

The decline of profit and interest does not bring on the downfall, but the narrowing of the capitalist class. Every year small capitalists are expelled from it and consigned to the same death-struggle in which the small dealer, the small producer, the small farmer, the small concerns generally, are engaged—a death-struggle that may be more or less protracted, but which will finally end for them, or for their children, with downfall into the proletariat. Their efforts to escape their fate only hasten their ruin.

One often wonders at the large number of simpletons whom any knave can allure to intrust him with their money upon the promise of high interest. Those people are, as a rule, not the fools they seem; fraudulent undertakings are the last straws at which sinking capitalists grasp, in the desperate hope of making their small capital remunerative. It is not so much greed as the fear of poverty that blinds them.

7. The Growth of Large Production. Syndicates and Trusts.

Side by side with the competitive struggle between individual and capitalist production rages the competitive struggle between large and small capitalists. Every day brings forth a new invention or a new discovery which increases the productivity of labor. Each of these renders useless, to a smaller or greater extent, former machines, and compels the introduction of new ones, often also the enlargement of establishments. The capitalist, who, at such a pinch, has not the requisite capital at his command, becomes, sooner or later, unable to hold his own in the competitive struggle and goes down, or is forced, at considerable loss, to invest his capital in some smaller industry not yet seized upon by more powerful capitalists than himself. In this way competition in large industry causes over-stocking of capital in small industry, and thereby renders the competition between the small capitalists all the more fierce and their ruin all the more rapid.

The industries conducted on a large scale constantly expand. Establishments that once counted their workmen by hundreds become giant concerns that employ thousands of hands. Day by day the small business establishments disappear; the industrial development, instead of increasing, steadily decreases the number of individual enterprises.

Nor is this all. The industrial development leads steadily to the concentration of more and more capitalist undertakings into a single hand, be that the hand of a single capitalist, or of a combination of capitalists who legally constitute one person—the syndicate, the trust.

The paths that lead to this are manifold.

One of them is opened by the anxiety of the capitalist to exclude competition. Competition has been shown to be the mainspring of the modern system of production; indeed, it is the mainspring of all production of merchandise, i. e., production for sale. Nevertheless, however necessary competition is for the production of merchandise in general, there is no capitalist but is anxious to see his own goods free from competition in the market. If he is the sole possessor of goods for which there is a·demand, if he has a monopoly of them, he can send their pricees far above their actual value; then those who need his goods will be wholly dependent upon him. Where several sellers of the same goods appear in the market, they can establish a monopoly only by combining in such a way that they virtually become one seller. Such combines—rings, syndicates, trusts—are the sooner and more easily brought about the smaller the number of competitors whose conflicting interests are to be harmonized.

In so far as the capitalist system expands the market and increases the number of competitors in it, it makes difficult the formation of monopolies in production and commerce. But in every branch of capitalist industry the moment arrives, sooner or later, when its further development implies the lessening of the number of establishments engaged in it. From that moment on the march is rapid toward the syndicate and the trust. The time when, in a given country, the syndicate can ripen into a trust may be hastened through the protection of its domestic market against foreign competitors by a high tariff. In such a case the number of competitors is diminished and the domestic producers can more easily come together, establish a monopoly, and, thanks to "Protection of home industry," fleece the national consumer to their hearts' content.

During the last twenty years the number of

trusts, through which the price and production of certain wares is "regulated," has increased greatly, especially in "protected" countries, such as the United States, France and Germany. The trust, once formed, the several concerns that have combined constitute virtually only one concern, under the guidance of a single head.

The articles most necessary for the development of production, such as coal and iron, are the ones that become the first subjects of syndicates and trusts. Combinations usually extend their influence far beyond the monopolized industries themselves; they render the whole machinery of production dependent upon a few monopolists.

Simultaneously with the effort to bring together the several establishments of one industry into a single hand, there also develops the effort of the several establishments engaged in different branches of industry, but one of which furnishes either the raw material or the machinery needed by the others, to unite under one management. It is a common thing to see railroad lines owning their own coal mines and locomotive works; sugar manufacturers raise a part of their own cane or beets; the producer of potatoes establish his own whisky distillery, etc.

There is still a third way, and that the simplest, by which several establishments are merged into one.

We have seen how important are the functions of the capitalist under the present system of production; under the system of private property in the means of production, large production is possible only as capitalist production. Under this system it is necessary, in order that production may be carried on smoothly, that the capitalist take the field with his capital and apply it effectively.

At the same time, the larger a capitalist undertaking becomes, the more necessary it is for the capitalist to relieve himself of a part of his increasing duties, either by passing them over to other capitalist concerns, or to some employe whom he engages to attend to his business. Of coures, it makes no difference in the industrial process whether these functions are performed by an employe or by the capitalist himself; these functions produce no value when performed by the capitalist and they produce no value when performed by the employe. The capitalist, consequently, must now pay for them out of his surplus. This is another means by which the surplus of the capitalist, and accordingly his profits, are lowered.

While the growth of an enterprise forces the capitalist to relieve himself by the employment of lieutenants, it, at the same time, through the increasing surplus it yields, reduces the expense of the change. The larger the surplus, the more functions can the capitalist transfer to his employes, until finally he relieves himself of all his functions; so that there remains to him only the care as to how to invest profitably that portion of his profits that he does not need for personal consumption.

The number of concerns in which this final stage has been reached grows from year to year.

This is shown clearly by the increase of stock companies, in which even the dullest intellect can see that the person of the capitalist cuts no figure, and the only thing of importance is his capital.

Some have imagined that they saw in the rise of stock companies a means whereby to render accessible to the small holders the benefits of large production. But the stock company, like credit, of which it is only a special form, is rather a means to place at the disposal of the large capitalist the property of the small holders.

Just as soon as a branch of industry can dispense with the person of the capitalist, everyone can engage in it, whether or not he knows anything of the business, provided only he possesses the necessary funds to buy stock. Owing to this fact a capitalist is able to unite in his own hands industries that are wholly disconnected. Stock companies are easily acquired by a large capitalist; all he needs to do is to secure possession of the majority of the stock, and the concern becomes dependent upon him and subject to his interests.

Finally, it must be observed that large masses of capital grow faster than the small ones, for the larger the capital, the larger, also, other things being equal, will be the profits, the smaller proportionately will be the quantity which the capitalist will consume personally, and the larger the portion which he can add to his previous investments as fresh capital. The capitalist whose business yields him a yearly income of $10,000 will be able to live but modestly according to capitalist ideas. On the other hand, the capitalist whose business is large enough to yield him $100,000 annually, may, even though he were to spend upon himself five times as much as the previous one, add annually $60,000, *i. e.*, three-fifths of his profits, to his previous capital. While the small capitalists are compelled to struggle harder and harder for their existence, the large accumulations in the hands of the large capitalists swell faster and faster and within a short time reach immense proportions.

To summarize: The growth of large establishments, the rapid increase of large fortunes, the steady decrease in the number of establishments, the steady concentration of different concerns in one hand,—all these make it evident that the tendency of the capitalist system of production is to concentrate in the hands of an ever smaller number the instruments of production, which have become the monopoly of the capitalist class. The final result must be the concentration of all the instruments of production in the hands of one person or one stock company, to be used as private property and be disposed of at will; the whole machinery of production will be turned into a gigantic concern subject to a single master. The private ownership of the means of production leads, under the capitalist system, to its own destruction! Its development takes the ground from under itself. The moment the wage-workers constitute the bulk of the consumers, the products in which the surplus lies locked up become unsalable, that is, valueless.

In point of fact, a state of things such as here

outlined would be as preposterous as it would be impossible. It will not, and cannot, come to that. The mere approach to such conditions would increase to such an extent the sufferings, antagonisms and contradictions in society, that they would become unbearable and society would fall to pieces, even if a different turn were not previously given to the development. But although such a condition of things will never be completely reached, we are rapidly steering in that direction. At the same time that, on the one hand, the concentration of separate capitalist undertakings in few hands is progressing rapidly, on the other hand, the interdependence of seemingly independent concerns increases as the inevitable result of the division of labor. This mutual dependence becomes, however, constantly more one-sided, for the small capitalists grow ever more dependent on the big ones. Just as most of those workers who are now engaged in home industries and who seem to be independent are in fact wage-workers under some capitalist, so also is many a small capitalist who apparently enjoys independence tributary to other capitalists, and many a seemingly independent capitalist concern is, in fact, but an appendage of some gigantic capitalist establishment.

At the same time that the economic dependence of the bulk of our population upon the capitalist class is on the increase, there is also an increasing dependence within the capitalist class itself of a majority of its members upon a small set whose numbers become smaller, but whose power, because of their wealth, becomes greater.

But dependence brings no more security to the capitalist than to the proletarians, the small traders and producers. On the contrary, it means to him what it does to all the others; with his dependence increases also the uncertainty of his situation. The smaller capitalists, of course, suffer most, but even the largest accumulations of capital afford no absolute certainty.

Some of the causes of the increasing insecurity of capitalist undertakings we have already touched upon. One of these, the sensitiveness of the whole system to outward influences, is on the increase. In proportion as it draws sharper the antagonism between the classes; in proportion as it swells more and more the masses it arraigns against each other; in proportion as it places in the hands of each increasingly powerful weapons; the capitalist system of production multiplies the occasions for disturbances and increases the damages which these disturbances bring about. Furthermore, it is not only the surplus withheld by the capitalist that the growing productivity of labor increases; it increases also the quantity of goods that are thrown upon the market. Along with the exploitation of labor grows the competition among capitalists, which becomes a bitter contest of each against all. Together with this goes a steady revolution in the technical methods of production. New inventions and discoveries are incessantly made which render valueless existing machinery and make superfluous, not only individual workers, not only individual machines, but often whole establishments or even whole branches of industry.

No capitalist can depend on the future; none can say with certainty whether he will be able to keep what he has and to leave it to his children.

The capitalist class itself is splitting up into two sets. The one, which increases steadily, is superfluous to industrial life; it has nothing to do but squander the growing quantity of surplus which flows into its hands. The other set, which consists of those who have not yet become superfluous in their establishments, decreases steadily, but in proportion to this decrease the cares and burdens of their situation grow heavier upon them. While the former set is degenerating in wasteful idleness, the latter is wearing itself out in the competitive struggle.

To both the specter of uncertainty is a growing menace. The modern system of production does not allow even the exploiters, even those who monopolize all its tremendous advantages, to enjoy their booty to the full.

8. Industrial Crises.

Great as is the uncertainty for all classes under our usual conditions, it is further increased by the crises which are periodically brought on, with the certainty of natural law, the moment production reaches a certain stage.

The importance which these crises have assumed during the last decades and the general confusion of thought that prevails concerning them justifies special attention.

The great modern crises which convulse the world's markets arise from overproduction.

which, in its turn, arises from the planlessness that inevitably characterizes our system of commodity production. Overproduction, in the sense of more being produced than is actually needed, may occur under any system. But it could, as a matter of course, cause no injury so long as the producers produce for the satisfaction of their own wants. If, for instance, in the generation gone by, a farmer's crop of grain happened to be larger than he needed, he stored up the grain against poorer years, and when his barn was full, he would feed his cattle with the residue, or, at worst, let it lie and spoil.

It is otherwise with the modern system of commodity production. In the first place, when the system is once well-developed, no one produces for himself, but for someone else; everyone must buy what he needs. Moreover, the total production of society is not carried on in a systematic way; on the contrary, it is left to each producer to estimate for himself the demand there may be for the goods which he produces. In the second place, just as soon as the modern system of production has outgrown its first stage, no one except the producer of coinable metals can buy before he has sold. These are the two roots out of which grows the crisis.

For the illustration of this fact let the simplest example serve. At a market-place let there come together an owner of money, say a gold-digger with twenty dollars in gold, a wine-merchant with a cask of wine, a weaver with a bale of cloth, and a miller with a sack of flour. To simplify the case, let the value of each of these goods be equal to twenty dollars, and let it be assumed that each has correctly estimated the needs of the other. The wine-merchant sells his wine to the gold-digger, and with the twenty dollars he receives for it purchases the cloth in the hands of the weaver; and, lastly, the weaver invests the proceeds of his cloth in the purchase of the sack of meal. Each will go home satisfied.

Next year these four meet again, each calculating upon the same demand for his goods as before. Let it be assumed that the gold-digger does not despise the merchant's wine, but that the wine-merchant either has no need of the cloth, or requires the money to pay a debt, and prefers wearing a torn shirt to purchasing new material. In that case the wine-merchant keeps in his pocket the twenty dollars and goes home. In vain does the weaver wait for a customer, and for the same reason that he waits, the miller is also disappointed. The weaver's family may be hungry, he may crave the flour in the miller's hands, but he has produced cloth for which there is no demand, and for the same reason that the cloth has become superfluous, the flour also is rendered "superfluous." Neither the weaver nor the miller has any money, neither can purchase what he wants; what they have produced now appears as excessive production. Furthemore, the same is the case with all other goods which have been produced for their use and which they stand in need of; to carry the illustration a little further, the table produced by the joiner and needed by the miller is "overproduced."

The essential features of an industrial crisis

are all present in this illustration. Of course, in reality, the crisis does not manifest itself at such a primitive stage of production. At the first stage of production of merchandise, production for sale, every producer produces more or less for self-consumption; production for sale constitutes in each family but a part of its total industry. The weaver and the miller of the illustration given above are each possessed of a patch of land and some cattle, and they can wait patiently until a purchaser for their commodities turns up. If the worst came to the worst, they could even manage to live without him.

Furthermore, in the first stages of production for sale the market is still small, it can easily be estimated; year in and year out, production and consumption, the whole social life of a community, keep on the even tenor of their way. In the small settlements of the past everyone knew everybody and was well-informed as to his wants and his purchasing capacity. The industrial activity of such places remained substantially the same from year to year; the number of producers, the productivity of labor, the quantity of products, the number of consumers, their wants, the money at their disposal—all of these changed but slowly, and each change was promptly observed and taken into consideration.

All this takes on a different aspect with the appearance of commerce. Under its influence production for self-consumption is crowded ever more to the rear; the individual producers of the goods for sale, and to a greater extent the dealers, are more and more thrown for their support upon the sale of their goods, and, what is more important, upon their prompt sale. The prevention of the sale of a commodity, or even a delay in the sale, becomes ever more disastrous to the owner; it may even cause his ruin.

Through commerce the most various and widely separated markets are brought together; the general market is greatly extended, but it becomes correspondingly more difficult to control. This inconvenience is further increased by the appearance of one or more middlemen who squeeze themselves between the producers and consumers. Simultaneously with the development of trade and the means of communication the transportation of products has been facilitated; the slightest cause is sufficient to bring them together in great quantities at any point. All these causes combined render more and more uncertain the work of estimating the demand for, and supply of, commodities. The development of statistics does not remove this uncertainty. The whole economic life of society becomes constantly more dependent upon mercantile speculation, and the latter becomes ever more risky.

The merchant is a speculator from the start. Speculation was not invented at the exchange; it is a necessary function of the capitalist. By speculating, that is, by estimating in advance the demand for a commodity; by buying his goods where he can get them cheap, that is, where their supply is excessive; by selling them where they are dear, that is, where they are scarce, the merchant helps to bring some order into the chaos of the planless system of production that is carried on by individually independent concerns. But he is liable to err in his calculations, and all the more as he is not allowed much time to consider his ventures. He is not the only merchant in the world; hundreds and thousands of competitors lie in wait to profit by every favorable opportunity; whoever first espies it carries off the prize. Under such circumstances quickness is a necessity; it will not do to reflect long, to inquire much; the capitalist must venture. Yet he may lose. So soon as there is a great demand for a commodity in any market, it flows thither in large quantities until it exceeds the digestive powers of the market. Then prices tumble; the merchant must sell cheap, often at a loss, or seek another market with his goods. His losses in this operation may be large enough to ruin him.

Wherever the modern system of production for sale is well developed, any given market is either excessively or inadequately supplied. This may lead to the result that in response to some extraordinary cause, the overstocking of the market becomes so excessive that the losses of the merchants may be unusually heavy and a large number of them become unable to meet their liabilities; that is, they fail. Under such circumstances we have a first-class commercial crisis.

So long as small production was the leading form of industry, the extent and intensity of commercial crises could not but be limited. Whatever the call, it was not then possible to increase rapidly the total amount of commodities at any one place. Under the regime of hand-work or small industry, production is not capable of any

considerable extension. It cannot be extended
by the employment of a larger number of workmen, for, under ordinary circumstances, it em-
ploys all the members of a community that are
at its disposal. It can be extended only by making heavier the burden of toil borne by the
worker—lengthening his hours of work, depriving him of holidays, etc. ; but in the good old days
the independent mechanic and farmer, who were
not yet crowded by the competition of large production, had no inclination for this. Finally, even
if they submitted to such imposition, it made little
difference to production, for the productivity of
labor was comparatively small.

This changes with the rise of capitalist large
production. This system not only develops all
the means that enable commerce to swamp any
market with goods to a degree never dreamt of
before, it not only expands the separate markets
into a world-market that embraces the whole
globe, it not only multiplies the number of the
middlemen between the producer and the consumer, it also enables production to respond to
every call of trade and to extend by leaps and
bounds.

At present, the very fact that the workmen are
wholly subject to the capitalist—that he can, virtually at will, lengthen their hours of work, sus-
pend their Sundays, limit their night rest—enables him to increase production at a more rapid
pace than was formerly possible. Furthermore,
today one single hour of overwork means, with
the present productivity of labor, an increase of
production immensely larger than in the days of

handicraft. Thanks to credit, capital has become a very elastic quantity. A brisk trade increases confidence, draws money out upon the street, shortens the time requisite for the turning over of capital and, accordingly, increases its effectiveness. But most important of all, capital has permanently at its disposal a large reserve army of workmen—the unemployed. The capitalist is thus able at any time to expand his establishment, to employ additional workmen, to increase his production rapidly and to profit to the utmost by every favorable opportunity.

It has been shown that under the rule of large production industrial capital steps ever more to the front and takes control of the whole capitalist mechanism. But within the circle of capitalist production itself special branches of industry take the lead, as for instance, the iron and spinning industries. The moment any of these receives a special impetus—be it through the opening of new markets in China, or the undertaking of extensive railroad lines—not only does it expand rapidly, but it imparts the impetus it has received to the whole industrial organism. Capitalists enlarge their establishments, start new ones, increase the consumption of raw and auxiliary materials and employ new hands; simultaneously with all this, rent, profit and wages go up. The demand for goods increases, all industries begin to feel the industrial prosperity. At such times it looks as if every undertaking must prosper; confidence becomes blind, credit grows boundless. Whoever has money seeks to turn it into capital to make it profitable. Industrial giddiness takes possession of all.

In the meantime, production has greatly increased and the originally increased demand upon the market has been satisfied. Nevertheless, production does not stop. One producer does not know what the other is about, and even if, in a lucid interval, misgivings may arise in the mind of some capitalist, they are soon smothered by the necessity of profiting by the opportunity in order not to be left behind in the competitive race. "The devil takes the hindmost." In the meantime, the disposal of the increased quantity of goods becomes ever more difficult, the warehouses fill up. Yet the hurly-burly goes on. Then comes the moment when one of the mercantile establishments must pay for the goods received from the manufacturer months before. The goods are yet unsold; the debtor has the goods, but no money; he cannot meet his obligations and fails. Next comes the turn of the manufacturer. He also has contracted debts that fall due; as his debtor cannot pay him, he, too, is ruined. Thus one bankruptcy follows another until a general collapse ensues. The recent blind confidence turns into an equally blind fear, the panic grows general, and the crash comes.

At such times the whole industrial mechanism is shaken to its very center; every establishment that is not planted upon the firmest ground goes to pieces. Misfortune overtakes not the fraudulent concerns alone, but all those which in ordinary times just managed to keep their heads above water. At such times the expropriation of the small farmers, small producers, small dealers and small capitalists goes on rapidly. As a matter of course, those among the large capitalists who survive get a rich booty. For during a crisis two important things take place: first, the expropriation of the "small fry"; second, the concentration of production into fewer hands, and thereby the accumulation of large fortunes.

Few, if any, can tell whether they will survive the crisis. All the horrors of the modern system of production, the uncertainty of a livelihood, want, prostitution and crime, reach at such times alarming proportions. Thousands perish from cold and hunger because they have produced too much clothing, too much food, and too many houses! It is at such seasons that the fact becomes most glaring that the modern productive powers are becoming more and more irreconcilable with the system of production for sale, and that private ownership in the means of production is growing into a greater and greater curse— first, for the class of the propertyless, and then for that of the property holders themselves.

Some political economists have declared that the trust would do away with the crisis. This is false.

The regulation of production by large syndicates or trusts presupposes above all things their control of all branches of industry and the organization of these upon an international basis in all countries over which the capitalist system of production extends. But international trusts are difficult to organize and more difficult to hold together; so it is seldom that a trust becomes powerful enough to regulate international trade and avert a crisis. With regard to overproduction, the principal mission of the trust is not to check it, but to shift its evil consequences from the shoulders of capitalists upon those of workmen and consumers.

But let it be assumed that eventually the leading industries have been successfully organized into well-disciplined, international trusts. What would be the result? Competition among capitalists would be removed in one direction only. The more completely competition disappears among the producers in one branch of industry, the greater becomes the antagonism between them and the producers of other commodities, who, as consumers, need the products of the trust, in short, complete international trustification would cause the capitalist class to be divided no longer into competing individuals, but into hostile groups, who would wage war to the knife against one another.*

Only when all trusts are joined into one and the whole machinery of production of all capitalist nations is concentrated in a few hands, that is, when private property in the means of production has virtually come to an end, can the trust abolish the crisis. On the contrary, from a certain stage on in industrial development, the crisis is inevitable so long as private property in the means of production continues.

9. Chronic Overproduction.

Along with the periodical crises and their permanent manifestations, along with the recurring

---

*Note.—In America this stage of growth in the development of trusts has been reached in many industries or groups of industries.—Translator.

periods of overproduction and their accompaniments of loss of wealth and waste of force, there develops chronic overproduction and waste of energy.

The revolution in the machinery of production goes on uninterrupted; the fields that it invades are ever more numerous. Year after year new branches of industry are captured by capitalist large production, and, consequently, the productivity of labor grows incessantly, and at an ever increasing rate. Simultaneously with this the accumulation of new capital proceeds without interruption. The intenser the exploitation of the single laborer and the larger the number of the exploited laborers, the larger also grows the quantity of the surplus and the mass of wealth that the capitalist class can lay by and apply as capital. The capitalist system, therefore, cannot remain stationary; its constant expansion and the constant expansion of its market are a vital necessity to it; to stand still is death. While formerly, in the days of handicraft and small farming, the country produced year in and year out a quantity of wealth, which, as a rule, increased only with the increase of the population, the capitalist system, on the contrary, is from the start dependent on an incessant increase of production; every stoppage indicates a social malady which grows more painful the longer it lasts. Thus, together with the periodical incentives to increase of production brought on by the periodical extensions of the market, there is a permanent pressure in this direction inherent in the capitalist system of production itself. This pressure, instead of being brought on by the extension of the market, compels the latter to be pushed constantly further.

But there is a limit to the extension of the markets; there have been periods during the last thirty years when it has not gone on. True enough, the field over which capitalist production can extend itself is immense; it leaps over all local and national boundaries, it has the whole globe for its market. But capitalism has virtually reduced the size of the globe. Only a hundred years ago the market for capitalist industry was limited to the western part of Europe and certain coastlands and islands almost exclusively dominated by England. But such was the vigor and greed of the capitalists and so gigantic were the means at their disposal, that since then almost all countries on earth have been forced open, not to the products of England alone, but to those of all capitalist nations. Today there are hardly any other markets to be opened, except those from which little is to be fetched besides fever and blows.

The wonderful development of transportation renders from year to year a completer exploitation of the market possible; but this tendency is counteracted by the circumstance that the market steadily undergoes a change in those very countries whose population has reached a certain degree of civilization. Everywhere the introduction of the goods of capitalist large production extinguishes the domestic system of small production and transforms the industrial and agricultural laborers into proletarians. This produces two important results in all the markets that are counted upon to absorb the surplus products of capitalist industry: first, it lowers the purchasing power of the population and thereby counteracts the effect of the extension of the market; and, second, and more important, it lays there the foundation for the capitalist system of production by calling into existence a proletarian class. Thus capitalist large production digs its own grave. From a certain point onward in its development every new extension of the market means the rising of a new competitor. At present, capitalist large production in the United States, which is not quite a generation old, is engaged not only in the work of freeing itself from its European competitor, but in an endeavor to seize upon the market of the whole American continent. The still more youthful capitalist industry of Russia has started in to be the sole purveyor of the whole extensive territory owned by Russian in Europe and Asia. The East Indies, China, Japan, Australia are developing into industrial states that sooner or later will be able to supply their own wants. In short, the moment is drawing near when the markets of the industrial countries can no longer be extended and will begin to contract. But this would mean the bankruptcy of the whole capitalist system.

For some time past the extension of the market has not kept pace with the requirements of capitalist production. The latter is, consequently, more and more hampered and finds it increasingly difficult to develop fully the productive powers that it possesses. The intervals of prosperity become ever shorter; the length of the crises ever longer.

Hence the quantity of the means of production that either cannot be turned to sufficient use or is forced to remain wholly unused, is on the increase; the quantity of wealth that goes to waste is greater and greater; the quantity of labor power compelled to lie idle is ever more appalling. Under this last head belong not only the swarms of unemployed who are rapidly growing into a threatening social danger; under it must also be numbered, first, that ever-increasing crew of social parasites who, finding all avenues of productive work closed to them, try to eke out a miserable existence through a variety of occupations, most of which are wholly superfluous and not a few injurious to society—such as middlemen, saloonkeepers, agents, drummers, etc.; second, that stupendous mass of humanity of all degrees that may be designated as "the slums," such as the cheats and swindlers of high and low grade, the criminals and prostitutes, together with their innumerable dependents; third, the swarms of those who fasten upon the possessing classes in the capacity of personal servants; finally, there is the great body of soldiers, for the steady increase of armies during the last twenty years would not have been possible without the overproduction which has set free so large a part of the world's labor-power.

The capitalist system begins to suffocate in its own surplus; it becomes constantly less able to endure the full unfolding of the productive powers which it has created. Constantly more creative forces must be idle, ever greater quantities of products be wasted, if it is not to go to pieces altogether.

The introduction of the capitalist system, that is, the replacing of small production, under which the instruments of labor were the property of the individual workers, with capitalist large production, under which the implements of labor became the private property of a few individuals and workmen were turned into propertyless proletarians, was the means whereby the productive powers of labor were immensely increased. To do this was the historic mission of the capitalist class. The sufferings inflicted upon the masses of human beings expropriated and exploited were terrible, but it fulfilled its mission. It was as much a historic necessity as the two cornerstones upon which it rose; first, the production of merchandise, that is, production for sale; next, the private ownership of the implements of labor.

But however necessary were the capitalist system and the conditions which produced it, they are no longer so. The functions of the capitalist class devolve ever more upon paid employes. The large majority of the capitalists have now nothing to do but consume what others produce. The capitalist today is as superfluous a human being as the feudal lord had become a hundred years ago.

Nay, more. Like the feudal lord of the eighteenth century, the capitalist class has today become a hindrance to further development. Private ownership in the implements of labor has long ceased to secure to each producer the product of his labor and to guarantee him freedom. Today, on the contrary, society is rapidly drifting to the point where the whole population of capitalist nations will be deprived of both property and freedom. What was once a foundation stone of society has become a means of tearing up all foundations: instead of a means of spurring society on to the highest development of its productive powers, it has become a means of compelling society more and more to waste its powers of production. So private property in the means of production has changed from what it originally was into its opposite, not only for the small producer, but for society as a whole. From a motive power of progress it has become a cause of social degradation and bankruptcy.

Today there is no longer any question as to whether the system of private ownership in the means of production shall be maintained. Its downfall is certain. The only question to be answered is: Shall the system of private ownership in the means of production be allowed to pull society with itself down into the abyss; or shall society shake off that burden and then, free and strong, resume the path of progress which the evolutionary law prescribes to it?

IV. THE COMMONWEALTH OF THE FUTURE.

1. Social Reform and Social Revolution.

"Private ownership in the instruments of production, once the means of securing to the producer the ownership of his product, has to-day become the means of expropriating the farmer, the artisan, and the small trader, and of placing the non-producers—capitalists and landlords—in possession of the products of labor. Only the conversion of private ownership of the means of production—the land, mines, raw materials, tools, machines and the means of transportation and communication—into social ownership and the conversion of commodity production into socialist production, carried on for and by society, can production on a large scale and the ever-increasing productivity of social labor be changed from a source of misery and oppression for the exploited classes, into one of well-being and harmonious development."—Article 5, Erfurter Program.

The productive forces that have been generated in capitalist society have become irreconcilable with the very system of property upon which it is built. The endeavor to uphold this system of property renders impossible all further social development, condemns society to stagnation and decay—a decay that is accompanied by the most painful convulsions. ˙

Every further perfection in the powers of production increases the contradiction that exists between these and the present system of property. All attempts to remove this contradiction, or even to soften it down, without interfering with property, have proved vain, and must continue so to prove as often as attempted.

For the last hundred years thinkers and statesmen among the possessing classes have been trying to prevent the threatened downfall of the system of private property in the instruments of production, that is to say, to prevent revolution. Social reform is the name they give to their perpetual tinkerings with the industrial mechanism for the sake of removing this or that ill effect of private property in the means of production, at least of softening its edge, without touching private property itself. During the last hundred years manifold cures have been recommended and tried; it is now hardly possible to imagine any new receipe in this line. All the so-called "latest" panaceas of our social quacks which are to heal the old social evils quickly, without pain and without expense, are, upon closer inspection, discovered to be but a revival of old devices, all of which have been tried before in other places and found worthless. We pronounce these reforms inoperative in so far as they propose to remove the growing contradictions between the powers of production and the existing system of property and at the same time strive to uphold and confirm the latter. But we do not mean that the social revolution—the abolition of private property in the means of production—will be accomplished of itself, that the irresistible, inevitable course of evolution will do the work without the assistance of man; nor yet that all social reforms are worthless and that nothing is left to those who suffer from the contradiction between the modern powers of production and the system of property but idly to fold their arms and patiently to wait for its abolition.

When we speak of the irresistible and inevitable nature of the social revolution, we presuppose that men are men and not puppets; that they are beings endowed with certain wants and impulses, with certain physical and mental powers which they will seek to use in their own interest. Patiently to yield to what may seem unavoidable is not to allow the social revolution to take its course, but to bring it to a standstill.

When we declare the abolition of private property in the means of production to be unavoidable, we do not mean that some fine morning the exploited classes will find that, without their help, some good fairy has brought about the revolution. We consider the breakdown of the present social system to be unavoidable, because we know that the economic evolution inevitably brings on conditions that will compel the exploited classes to rise against this system of private ownership. We know that this system multiplies the number and the strength of the exploited, and diminishes the number and strength of the exploiting, classes, and that it will finally lead to such unbearable conditions for the mass of the population that they will have no choice but to go down into degradation or to overthrow the system of private property.

Such a revolution may assume many forms, according to the circumstances under which it takes place. It is by no means necessary that it be accompanied with violence and bloodshed. There are instances in history when the ruling classes were either so exceptionally clear-sighted or so particularly weak and cowardly that they submitted to the inevitable and voluntarily abdicated.   Neither is it necessary that the social revolution be decided at one blow; such probably was never the case.   Revolutions prepare themselves by years or decades of economic and political struggle; they are accomplished amidst constant ups and downs sustained by the conflicting classes and parties; not infrequently they are interrupted by long periods of reaction.

Nevertheless, however manifold the forms may be which a revolution may assume, never yet was any revolution accomplished without vigorous action on the part of those who suffered most under the existing conditions.

When, furthermore, we declare that those social reforms which stop short of the overthrow of the present system of property are unable to abolish the contradictions which the present economic development has produced, we by no means imply that all struggles on the part of the exploited against their present sufferings are useless within the framework of the existing social order.   Nor do we claim that they should patiently endure all the ill-treatment and all the forms of exploitation which the capitalist system may decree to them, or that so long as they are at all exploited, it matters little how.   What we do mean is that the exploited classes should not overrate the social reforms, and should not imagine that through them the existing conditions can be rendered satisfactory. The exploited classes should carefully examine all the social reforms that are offered to them. Nine-tenths of the proposed reforms are not only useless, but positively injurious to the exploited classes. Most dangerous of all are those which, aiming at the salvation of the threatened social order, shut their eyes to the economic development of the last century. The working-men who take the field in favor of such schemes waste their energies in a senseless endeavor to revive the dead past.

Many are the ways in which the economic development may be influenced: it may be hastened and it may be retarded; its results may be made more, or less, painful; only one thing is impossible—to stop its course, or turn it back.

When, for instance, in the early stages of capitalism, the workers destroyed the machines, opposed woman's labor, and so on, their efforts were useless, and could not be otherwise. They arrayed themselves against a development that nothing could resist. Since then they have hit upon better methods whereby to shield themselves as much as possible against the injurious effects of capitalist exploitation. With their trade-unions and their political activities, each supplementing the other, they have in all civilized countries met with more or less success. But each of their successes, be it the raising of wages, the shortening of hours, the prohibition of child labor, the establishment of sanitary regulations, gives a new impulse to the economic development. For example it may have caused the capitalist to replace the dearer labor with machinery, or it may have forced up his pay-roll and thereby rendered the competitive struggle harder for the small capitalist, shortened his economic existence and hastened the concentration of capital.

Accordingly, however justifiable, or even necessary, it may be for the workmen to establish labor organizations to better their condition by lowering the hours of work and securing other equally wholesome changes, it would be a profound error to imagine that such reforms could delay the social revolution. Equally mistaken is the notion that one cannot admit the usefulness of social reforms without admitting that it is necessary to preserve society upon its present basis. On the contrary, reforms may be supported from the revolutionary standpoint and because, as has been shown, they hasten the course of events and because, so far from doing away with the suicidal tendencies of the capitalist system, they rather strengthen them.

The turning of the people into proletarians, the concentration of capital in the hands of a few, who rule the whole economic life of capitalist nations, none of these cruel and revolting effects of the capitalist system can be checked by any reform that is based upon the existing system of property, however far-reaching such reform may be.

2. Private Property and Common Property.

Indeed, there can no longer be any question as to how private property in the instruments of production is to be preserved; the only question is what shall, or rather must, take its place. It is not a question of making an invention but of dealing with a fact. We have as little choice in the matter of the system of property that shall be instituted as we have in the matter of preserving the present one or throwing it overboard.

The same economic development that forces on us the question, What shall we put in the place of the system of private ownership in the means of production? brings with it the conditions that answer the question. The new system of property lies latent in the old. To become acquainted with it we must turn, not to our personal leanings and desires, but to the facts that surround us.

Whoever understands the conditions that are requisite for the present system of production knows what system of property those conditions will demand when the existing system of property ceases to be possible. Private property in the instruments of production has its root in small production. Individual production makes individual ownership necessary. Large production, on the contrary, means co-operation, social production. In large production the individual does not work alone, but a large number of workers, the whole commonwealth, work together to produce a whole. Accordingly, the modern instruments of production are extensive and powerful. It has become wholly impossible that every single worker should own his own instruments of production. Once the present stage is reached by large production, it admits of but two systems of ownership.

First, private ownership by the individual in the means of production used by co-operative labor; that means the existing system of capitalist production with its train of misery and exploitation as the portion of the workers and suffocating abundance as the portion of the capitalist.

Second, ownership by the workers in common of the instruments of production; that means a co-operative system of production and the extinction of the exploitation of the workers, who become masters of their own products and who themselves appropriate the surplus of which, under our system, they are deprived by the capitalist.

To substitute common, for private, ownership in the means of production, this it is that economic development is urging upon us with ever-increasing force.

3. Socialist Production.

The abolition of the present system of production means substituting production for use for production for sale.

Production for use may be of two forms:

First, individual production for the satisfaction of individual wants; and,

Second, social or co-operative production for the satisfaction of the wants of a commonwealth.

The first form of production has never been a general form of production. Man has always been a social being, as far back as we can trace

him. The individual has always been thrown
upon co-operation with others in order to satisfy
some of his principal wants; others had to work
for him and he, in turn, had to work for others.
Individual production for self-consumption has
always played a subordinate part; today it hardly
deserves mention.

Until the present system of production (production for sale) was developed, co-operative
production for common use was the leading
form; it is as old as production itself. If any
one system of production could be considered
better adapted than any other to the nature of
man, then co-operative production must be pronounced the natural one. In all probability for
every thousand years of production for sale, co-
operative production for use numbers tens of
thousands. The character, extent and power of
co-operative societies have changed along with
the instruments and methods of production which
they adopted. Nevertheless, whether such a
commonwealth was a horde or a tribe or any
other form of community, they all had certain essential features in common. Each satisfied its
own wants, at least the most vital ones, with
the product of its own labor; the instruments of
production were the property of the community;
its members worked together as free and equal
individuals according to some plan inherited or
devised, and administered by some power elected
by themselves. The product of such co-operative
labor was the property of the community and
was applied either to the satisfaction of common
wants, whether these were occasioned by produc-

tion or consumption, or were distributed among the individuals or groups which composed the community.

The well-being of such self-supporting communities or societies depended upon natural and personal conditions. The more fertile the territory they occupied, the more diligent, inventive and vigorous their members, the greater was the general well-being. Drouths, freshets, invasions by more powerful enemies, might afflict, or even destroy, them, but there was one visitation they were free from, the fluctuations of the market. With this they were either wholly unacquainted, or they knew it only in connection with articles of luxury.

Such co-operative production for use is nothing less than communistic or, as it is called today, socialist production. Production for sale can be overcome only by such a system. Socialist production is the only system of production possible when production for sale has become impossible.

This fact does not, however, imply that it is necessary to revive the dead past or to restore the old forms of community property or communal production. These forms were adapted to certain means of production; they were, and continue to be, inapplicable to more highly developed instruments of production. It was for that reason that they disappeared almost everywhere in the course of economic development at the approach of the system of production for sale, and wherever they did resist the latter, their effect was to interfere with the development of

productive powers. As reactionary and hopeless
as were the efforts to resist the system of production for sale, would be today any endeavor
to overthrow the present by a revival of the old
communal system.

The system of socialist production which has
become necessary, owing to the impending bankruptcy of our present system of production for
sale, will and must have certain features in common with the older systems of communal production, in so far, namely, as both are systems
of co-operative production for use. In the same
way, the capitalist system of production bears
some resemblance to the system of small and
individual production, which forms the transition between it and communal production; both
produce for sale. Just as the capitalist system
of production, as a higher development of commodity production, is different from small production, so will the form of social production,
that has now become necessary be different from
the former systems of production for use.

The coming system of socialist production will
not be the sequel to ancient communism; it will
be the sequel to the capitalist system of production, which itself develops the elements that are
requisite for the organization of its successor.
It brings forth the new people whom the new
system of production needs. But it also brings
forth the social organization which, as soon as
the new people have mastered it, will become the
foundation stone of the new system of production.

Socialist production requires, in the first place

the transformation of the separate capitalist establishments into social institutions. This transformation is being prepared for by the circumstance that the personality of the capitalist is steadily becoming more and more superfluous in the present mechanism of production. In the second place, it requires that all the establishments requisite for the satisfaction of the wants of the commonwealth be united into one large concern. How economic development is preparing the way for this by the steady concentration of capitalist concerns, has been explained in the foregoing chapter.

What must be the size of such a self-sufficing commonwealth? As the socialist republic is not an arbitrary creation of the brain, but a necessary product of economic development, the size of such a commanwealth cannot be predetermined. It must conform to the stage of social development out of which it grows. The higher the development that has been reached, the greater the division of labor that has been perfected, the more intercourse has developed between the producers—the larger will be the size of the commonwealth.

It is now nearly two hundred years since a well-meaning Englishman, John Bellers, submitted to the English Parliament a plan to end the misery which even then the capitalist system, young as it was, was spreading through the land. He proposed the establishment of communities that should produce everything that they needed, industrial as well as agricultural products. According to his plan, each community needed only from two hundred to three hundred workmen.

At that time handicraft was still the leading form of production; the capitalist system was still in the manufacturing stage; as yet there was no thought of the capitalist concern with its modern machinery.

A hundred years later the same idea was taken up anew, but considerably deepened and per-fected, by socialist thinkers. By that time the present factory system of mills and machinery had already begun; handicrafts were here and there disappearing; society had reached a higher stage, Accordingly, the communities which the socialists proposed at the beginning of the nine-teenth century for the purpose of removing the ills of the capitalist system were ten times larger than those proposed by Bellers (for instance, the phalansteries of Fourier).

In comparison with the ecnomic conditions of the time of Bellers, those which Fourier knew seemed wonderfully advanced; but from the point of view of a generation later these, in their turn, had become trivial. The machine was rest-lessly revolutionizing social life; it had expanded capitalist undertakings to such an extent that some of them already embraced whole nations in their operations; it had brought the several undertakings of a country into greater depend-ence upon one another so that they virtually con-stituted one industry; and it constantly tends to turn the whole economic life of capitalist nations into a single economic mechanism. The division and subdivision of labor is carried on further and further; the several industries apply themselves more and more to the production of special articles only; and what is more, to their production for the whole world; and the size of these establishments, some of which count their workmen by thousands, becomes constantly larger.

Under such circumstances, a community designed to satisfy its wants and embracing all the requisite industries, must have dimensions very different from those of the socialist colonies planned at the beginning of the nineteenth century. Among the social organizations in existence today there is but one that has the requisite dimensions, that can be used as the requisite field, for the establishment and development of the Socialist or Co-operative Commonwealth, and that is the modern state.

Indeed, so great is the development that production has reached in some industries and so intimate have become the connections between the several capitalist nations that one might almost question whether the limits of the state are sufficiently inclusive to contain the Co-operative Commonwealth.

Nevertheless, there is something else to be taken into account. The present expansion of international intercourse is due, not so much to the existing conditions of production as to the existing condition of exploitation. The greater the extension of capitalist production in a country and the intenser the exploitation of the working class, the larger also, as a rule, is the surplus of products that cannot be consumed in the country itself and that, consequently, must be sent abroad. If the population of the country have not themselves the means to buy the staples which they produce, the capitalists go with their products in search of foreign customers, whether or not the population of their own country stand in need of the products. The capitalists are after purchasers, not after consumers. This explains the horrible phenomenon that Ireland and India export large quantities of wheat during a famine; recently, during the frightful famine in Russia, the exportation of wheat by the Russian capitalists could be checked only by an imperial order. When exploitation shall have ceased, and production for use shall have taken the place of production for sale, exportation and importation of products from one state to another will fall off greatly.

The existing commerce between the several nations will not entirely disappear. The division of labor has been carried on so far, the market which certain giant industries require for their products has become so extensive, and, on the other hand, so many commodities,—supplied only by international commerce,—coffee, for instance—have become necessities, that it seems impossible for any Co-operative Commonwealth, even though co-extensive with a nation, to satisfy all its wants with its own products. Some sort of exchange of products between one nation and another is sure to continue. Such exchange will not, however, endanger the economic independence and safety of the several nations so long as they produce all that is actually necessary and exchange with one another superfluities only. A co-operative commonwealth co-extensive with the nation could produce all that it requires for its own preservation.

This dimension would by no means be unalterable. The modern nation is but a product and tool of the capitalist system of production; it grows with that system, not only in power, but also in extent. The domestic market is the safest for the capitalist class of every country. It is the easiest to maintain and to exploit. In proportion as the capitalist system develops, so also grows the pressure on the part of the capitalist class in every nation for an extension of its political boundaries. The statesman who maintained that modern wars are no longer manifestations of dynastic, but of national, aspirations was not far from the truth, provided one understands by national aspirations the aspirations of the capitalist class. Nothing so much injures the vital interests of the capitalists of any nation as a reduction of their territory. The capitalist class of France would long ago have pardoned Germany the $1,250,000,000 which she demanded as an indemnity for the war of 1870, but can never pardon the annexation of Alsace-Lorraine.

All modern nations feel the necessity of extending their boundaries. This is easiest for the United States, which will soon actually control all America, and for England, which is enabled by its sea power to expand the extent of its colonies without interruption. Russia also enjoyed at one time great advantages in this respect, but the limits of her aggrandizement seem to have been reached; she is bounded on all sides by

nations which resist her advancement. Worst
off are the nations of continental Europe in this
respect; they, as well as others, require terri-
torial expansion, but they are so closely hemmed
in by one another that none can grow except at
the expense of some other. The colonial policy
of these states affords inadequate relief to the
need of expansion caused by their capitalist
system of production. This situation is the most
powerful cause of the militarism which has
turned Europe into a military camp. There are
but two ways out of this intolerable state of
things: either a gigantic war that shall destroy
some of the existing European states, or the
union of them all in a federation.

This is enough to show that every modern
state has the desire to expand in response to the
demands of economic development. In this way
each is seeing to it that its boundaries become
sufficiently extensive to sat`sfy the needs of the
coming co-operative commonwealth.

4. The Economic Significance of the State.

All communities have had economic functions
to fulfill! This must, self-evidently, have been the
case with the original communist societies which
we encounter at the threshold of history. In
proportion as individual small production, private
ownership in the means of production, and production for sale underwent their successive development, a number of social functions came
into existence, the fulfillment of which either exceeded the power of the individual industries, or
were from the start recognized as too important

to be handed over to the arbitrary conduct of individuals. Along with the care for the poor, the young, the old, the infirm (schools, hospitals, poorhouses), the community reserved the functions of promoting and regulating commerce— i. e., building highways, coining money, superintending highways—and the management of certain general and important matters pertaining to production. In mediaeval society these several functions devolved upon the towns and sometimes upon religious corporations. The mediaeval state was little concerned with such functions. All this changed as the state took on its modern form, that is, became the state of office-holders and soldiers, the tool of the capitalist class. Like all previous states, the modern state is the tool of class rule. It could not, however, fulfill its mission and satisfy the needs of the capitalist class without either dissolving, or depriving of their independence, those economic institutions which lay at the foundation of the pre-capitalist social system, and taking upon itself their functions. Even in places where the modern state tolerated the continuance of mediaeval organizations, these fell into decay and became less and less able to fulfill their functions. These functions became, however, broader and broader with the development of the capitalist system; they grew with such rapidity that the state was gradually compelled to assume even those functions which it cares least to trouble itself about. For instance, the necessity of taking over the whole system of charitable and educational institutions has become so pressing upon the state that it has in most cases surrendered to this necessity. From the start it assumed the function of coining money; since then, forestry, care of the water supply, building of roads, come constantly more under its jurisdiction.

There was a time when the capitalist class, in its self-confidence, imagined it could free itself from the economic activities of the state; the state should only watch over their safety at home and abroad, keep the proletarians and foreign competitors in check, but keep its hands off the whole economic life. The capitalist class had good reasons for desiring this. However great the power of the capitalists, the power of the state had not always shown itself as subservient as they wished. Even where the capitalist class had virtually no competitor with whom to dispute the overlordship, and where, accordingly, the power of the state showed itself friendly, the office-holders often became disagreeable friends to deal with.

The hostility of the capitalist class to the interference of the state in the economic life of a country came to the surface first in England, where it received the name of the "Manchester School." The doctrines of that school were the first weapons with which the capitalist class took the field against the socialist-labor movement. It is therefore no wonder that the opinion took hold of many a socialist workingman that a supporter of the Manchester School and a capitalist were one and the same thing and that, on the other hand, Socialism and the interference of the state in the economic affairs of a country were identical. No wonder that such workingmen believed that to overthrow the Manchester School was to overthrow capitalism itself. Nothing less true. The Manchester teaching was never anything more than a teaching which the capitalist class played against the workingman or the government whenever it suited its purposes, but from the logical practice of which it has carefully guarded itself. Today the Manchester School no longer influences the capitalist class. The reason of its decline was the increasing force with which the economic and political development urged the necessity of the extension of the functions of the state.

These functions grew from day to day. Not only do those which the state assumed from the start become ever larger, but new ones are born of the capitalist system itself, of which the former generations had no conception and which affect ultimately the whole economic system. Formerly, statesmen were essentially diplomats and jurists; today they must, or should, be economists. Treaties and privileges, ancient researches and matters of precedent, are of little use in the solution of modern political problems; economic principles have become the leading arguments. What are today the chief matters with which statesmen concern themselves? Are they not finance, colonial affairs, tariff, protection and insurance of workingmen?

Nor is this all. The economic development forces the state, partly in self-defense, partly for the sake of better fulfilling its functions, partly also for the purpose of increasing its revenues, to take into its own hands more and more functions or industries.

During the Middle Ages the rulers derived their main income from their property in land; later, during the sixteenth, seventeenth and eighteenth centuries, their treasuries derived large accessions from the plundering of church and other estates. On the other hand, the need of money frequently compelled the rulers to sell their land to the capitalists. In most European countries even now, however, very considerable survivals of the former state ownership of land can be found in the domains of the crown and the state mines. Furthermore, the development of the military system added arsenals and wharves; the development of commerce added post-offices, railroads, and telegraphs; finally, the increasing demand for money on the part of the state has given birth, in European countries, to all manner of state monopolies.

While the economic functions and the economic power of the state are thus steadily increased, the whole economic mechanism becomes more and more complicated, more and more sensitive, and the separate capitalist undertakings become, as we have seen, proportionately more interdependent upon one another. Along with all this grows the dependence of the capitalist class upon the greatest of all their establishments,—the state or government. This increased dependence and interrelation increases also the disturbances and disorders which afflict the economic mechanism, for relief from all of which, the largest of existing economic powers, the state or government, is, with increasing frequency, appealed to by the capitalist class. Accordingly, in modern society the state is called upon more and more to step in and take a hand in the regulation and management of the economic mechanism, and ever stronger are the means placed at its disposal and employed by it in the fulfillment of this function. The economic omnipotence of the state, which appeared to the Manchester School as a socialist Utopia, has developed under the very eyes of that school into an inevitable result of the capitalist system of production itself.

5. State Socialism and the Social Democracy.

The economic activity of the modern state is the natural starting point of the development that leads to the Co-operative Commonwealth. It does not, however, follow that every nationalization of an economic function or of an industry is a step towards the Co-operative Commonwealth, and that the latter could be the result of a general nationalization of all industries without any change in the character of the state.

The theory that this could be the case is that of the state Socialists. It arises from a misunderstanding of the state itself. Like all previous systems of government, the modern state is preeminently an instrument intended to guard the interests of the ruling class. This feature is in no wise changed by its assumption of features of general utility which affect the interests not of the ruling class alone, but of the whole body politic. The modern state assumes these functions often simply because otherwise the interests of the ruling class would be endangered with those of society as a whole, but under no circumstances has it assumed, or could it ever assume, these functions in such a manner as to endanger the overlordship of the capitalist class.

If the modern state nationalizes certain industries, it does not do so for the purpose of restricting capitalist exploitation, but for the purpose of protecting the capitalist system and establishing it upon a firmer basis, or for the purpose of itself taking a hand in the exploitation of labor, increasing its own revenues, and thereby reducing the contributions for its own support which it would otherwise have to impose upon the capitalist class. As an exploiter of labor, the state is superior to any private capitalist. Besides the economic power of the capitalists, it can also bring to bear upon the exploited classes the political power which it already wields.

The state has never carried on the nationalizing of industries further than the interests of the ruling classes demanded, nor will it ever go further than that. So long as the property-holding classes are the ruling ones, the nationalization of industries and capitalist functions will never be carried so far as to injure the capitalists and landlords or to restrict their opportunities for exploiting the proletariat.

The state will not cease to be a capitalist institution until the proletariat, the working-class, has become the ruling class; not until then will it become possible to turn it into a co-operative commonwetlth.

From the recognition of this fact is born the

aim which the Socialist Party has set before it: to call the working-class to conquer the political power to the end that, with its aid, they may change the state into a self-sufficing co-operative commonwealth.

Socialists are frequently reproached with having no fixed aims, with being able to do nothing but criticize and with not knowing what to put in place of that which they would overthrow. Nevertheless, the fact remains that none of the existing parties has so well-marked and clear an aim as the Socialist Party. It may, indeed, be questioned whether the other political parties have any aims at all. They all hold to the existing order, although they all see that it is untenable and unendurable. Their programs contain nothing except a few little patches by which they hope and promise to make the untenable, tenable and the unendurable, endurable.

The Socialist Party, on the contrary, does not build on hopes and promises, but upon the unalterable necessity of economic development. Whoever declares these aims to be false should show in what respect the teachings of Socialist political economy are false. He should show that the theory of development from small to large production is false, that production is carried on today as it was a hundred years ago, that things are today as they have always been. Only he who could prove this is justified in the belief that things will continue as they are. But whoever is not featherbrained enough to believe that social conditions remain always the same, cannot reasonably suppose that the present conditions will continue forever. Can any other party than the Socialist Party point out to him what will and must take their place?

All other political parties live only in the present, from hand to mouth; the Socialist party is the only one which has a definite aim in the future, the only one whose present policy is dictated by a general, consistent purpose. Because they neither can nor will see, because they stubbornly persist in star-gazing they declare offhand that the Socialists know not what they want except to destroy the existing order.

6. The Structure of the Future State.

It is not our purpose to meet all the objections, misconceptions and misstatements with which the capitalist class strives to combat Socialism. It is profitless to attempt to enlighten malice and stupidity. Socialists could wear themselves to the bone in such an undertaking and never have done.

There is, however, one objection that should be met. It is important enough to merit thorough treatment, and its removal will make clearer the point of view and purpose of socialism.

Our opponents declare that the co-operative commonwealth cannot be considered practicable and cannot be the object of the endeavors of intelligent people until the plan is presented to the world in a perfected form, and has been tested and found feasible. They claim that no sensible man would start to built a house before he had perfected his plan, and before experts had approved of it; that least of all would he pull down his only dwelling before he knew what else to put in its place. Socialists are, accordingly, told that they must come out with their plan of a future state; if they refuse, it is a sign that they themselves have not much confidence in it.

This objection sounds very plausible, so plausible, indeed, that even among Socialists themselves many are of the opinion that the exposition of some such plan is necessary. Indeed, some plan seemed a necessary prerequisite as long as the laws of social evolution were unknown, and it was believed that social forms could be built up at will, like houses. People speak even to-day of "the social edifice."

Social evolution is a modern science. Formerly, economic development proceeded so slowly that it was barely noticeable. Mankind often remained centuries, and even thousands of years, at the same stage. There are neighborhoods in Russia where the agricultural implements still in use can scarcely be distinguished from those that we meet at the very threshhold of history. Hence it happened that the system of production in existence at a certain time seemed an unalterable arrangement to the people of that age. Their fathers and grandfathers had produced under that system and the conclusion was that their children would do likewise. Man naturally considered the social institutions into which he was born as permanent and ordained of God, and thought it was sacrilege to attempt innovations.

Great as the changes might be which were wrought by wars and class-struggles, they seemed to affect nothing but the surface of things. Such convulsions did, as a matter of course, affect the foundations also, but this fact was hardly noticeable to the individual observer who stood in the midst of such events. History is essentially nothing but a more or less faithful chronicle of events recorded by such spectators; hence history remains essentially superficial. Although one who takes a bird's-eye view of the thousands of years of antiquity can clearly perceive a social evolution, the average historian takes no notice of it.

Not until the age of capitalist production was reached did social evolution proceed at such a pace that men became conscious of it. Of course they first looked for the causes of this evolution on the surface. But one who sticks to the surface can see only the forces which determine the immediate course of progress, and these are not the changing conditions of production, but the changing ideas of men.

As the capitalist system developed it created among the persons who depended upon it, capitalists, proletarians, etc., new wants wholly different from those of the people connected with the feudal system of production. To these different wants there corresponded also different ideas of right and wrong, of necessities and luxuries, of usefulness and harm. In proportion as the capitalist system grew and the classes that had part in it became more marked, the ideas which corresponded to this system of production became clearer, asserted themselves in the government, and were felt in the social life, until finally the new classes that had been formed took possession of the state and shaped it agreeably to their own wants.

The philosophers who first endeavored to investigate the causes of social development thought they found them in the ideas of men. To a certain degree they recognized that these ideas sprang from material wants; but the fact still remained a secret to them that these wants changed from age to age, and that the changes were the results of alterations in economic conditions, that is, in the system of production. They started with the notion that the wants of man— "human nature"—were unchangeable. Hence they could see but one "true," "natural," "just" social system, because only one could correspond to the "true nature of man." All other social forms they pronounced the result of mental aberrations which came about only because mankind did not realize sooner what they needed; human judgment. it was thought, had been befogged, either, as some imagined, on account of the natural stupidity of man, or, as others maintained, on account of the willful machinations of kings or priests. Looked at from such a standpoint the development of society appears to be the result of a development of thought. The wiser men are, the quicker they are to discover the social forms that suit human nature, the juster and better does society become.

This is the theory of our so-called liberal thinkers. Wherever their influence is felt this view

prevails. As a matter of course the first social·
ists, who appeared at the beginning of the nineteenth century, were under the influence of it.
They, also, imagined that the institutions of the
capitalist state had sprung from the brain of
the philosophers of the previous century. But
it was clear to these socialists that the capitalist
system was not the perfect thing which the
eighteenth century expected. Accordingly this
system appeared to them as still falling short of
the true one; the philosophers of the eighteenth
century must have made a mistake somewhere.
The early socialists addressed themselves to the
task of finding the mistake, and, in their turn,
finding the true social system, that is, the one
that would perfectly suit human nature. They
realized that it was necessary to elaborate their
plan more carefully than any of their illustrious
predecessors had done, lest some untoward influence should nullify their work also. This
method of procedure was, moreover, dictated by
circumstances. The early socialists did not stand,
as did their predecessors, in the presence of a
social system near its downfall, nor did they have,
as did their predecessors, the encouragement of a
mighty class whose interests demanded the overthrow of the existing order. They could not present the social order for which they strove as inevitable, but only as desirable. It was a necessity
of their situation, then, to present their ideal
in as clear and tangible a form as possible to
the end that the mouths of people should water
after it, and none should entertain a doubt either
as to its practicability or desirability.

The adversaries of socialism have not got beyond the standpoint occupied by the social science of a hundred years ago. The only socialists they know and can understand are, accordingly, those early utopian socialists who started from the same premises as they themselves. The adversaries of socialism look upon the socialist commonwealth just as they would upon a capitalist enterprise, a stock company, for example, which is to be "started," and they refuse to take stock before it is shown in a prospectus that the concern will be practicable and profitable. Such a conception may have had its justification at the beginning of the nineteenth century; today, however, the socialist commonwealth no longer needs the endorsement of these gentlemen.

The capitalist social system has run its course; its dissolution is now only a question of time. Irresistible economic forces lead with the certainty of doom to the shipwreck of capitalist production. The substitution of a new social order for the existing one is no longer simply desirable, it has become inevitable.

Ever larger and more powerful grows today the mass of the propertyless workers for whom the existing system is unbearable; who have nothing to lose by its downfall, but everything to gain; who are bound—unless they are willing to go down with the society of which they have become the most important part—to call into being a social order that shall correspond to their interests.

These statements are not mere fancies; socialists have demonstrated them with the actual facts of our system of production. These facts are more eloquent and convincing than the most brilliant pictures of the future order could be. The best that such pictures can do is to show that the socialist commonwealth is not impossible. But they are bound to be defective; they can never cover all the details of social life; they will always leave some loophole through which an enemy can insinuate an objection. That, however, which is shown to be inevitable is thereby shown, not only to be possible, but to be the only thing possible. If indeed the socialist commonwealth were an impossibility, then mankind would be cut off from all further economic development. In that event modern society would decay, as did the Roman empire nearly two thousand years ago, and finally relapse into barbarism.

As things stand today capitalist civilization cannot continue; we must either move forward into socialism or fall back into barbarism.

In view of this situation it is wholly unnecessary to endeavor to move the enemies of socialism by means of a captivating picture. Anyone to whom the occurrences of the modern system of production do not loudly announce the necessity of the socialist commonwealth will be totally deaf to the praises of a system which does not yet exist and which he cannot realize nor understand.

Moreover, the construction of a plan upon which the future social order is to be built has become, not only purposeless, but wholly irreconcilable with the point of view of modern science. In the course of the nineteenth century a great revolution took place, not only in the economic world, but also in men's minds. Insight into the causes of social development has increased tremendously. As far back as the forties Marx and Engels showed—and from that time on every step in social science has proved it— that, in the last analysis, the history of mankind is determined, not by ideas, but by an economic development which progresses irresistibly, obedient to certain underlying laws and not to anyone's wishes or whims. In the foregoing chapters we have seen how it goes on; how it brings about new forms of production which require new forms of society; how it starts new wants among men which compel them to reflect upon their social condition, and to devise means whereby to adjust society to the new system in accordance with which production is carried on. For, we must always remember, this process of adjustment does not proceed of itself; it needs the aid of the human brain. Without thought, without ideas, there is no progress. But ideas are only the means to social development; the first impulse does not proceed from them, as was formerly believed, and as many still think; the first impulse comes from economic conditions.

Accordingly it is not the thinkers, the philosophers, who determine the trend of social progress. What the thinkers can do is to discover, to recognize, the trend; and this they can do in proportion to the clearness of their understanding of the conditions which preceded, but they can never themselves determine the course of social evo·lution.

And even the recognition of the trend of social progress has its limits. The organization of social life is most complex; even the clearest intellect finds it impossible to probe it from all sides and to measure all the forces at work in it with sufficient accuracy to enable him to foretell accurately what social forms will result from the joint action of all these forces.

A new social form does not come into existence through the activity of certain especially gifted men. No man or group of men can conceive of a plan, convince people by degrees of its utility, and, when they have acquired the requisite power, undertake the construction of a social edifice according to their plan.

All social forms have been the result of long and fluctuating struggles. The exploited have fought against the exploiting classes; the sinking reactionary classes against the progressive, revolutionary ones. In the course of these struggles the various classes have merged in all manner of combinations to battle with their opponents. The camp of the exploited at times contains both revolutionary and reactionary elements; the camp of the revolutionists may contain at times both exploiters and exploited. Within a single class different factions are frequently formed according to the intellect, the temperament, or the station of individuals or whole sections. And, finally, the power wielded by any single class has never been permanent; each has risen or fallen as its understanding of the surrounding conditions, the compactness and size of its organization, and its importance in the mechanism of production increased or diminished.

In the course of the fluctuating struggles of these classes the older social forms, which had become untenable, were pushed aside for new ones. The social order which took the place of the old was not always immediately the best possible. In order to have made it so the revolutionary class of each epoch would have had to be in possession of the sole political power and the most perfect understanding of their social conditions. As long as this was not the case, mistakes were inevitable. Not infrequently a new social order proved itself partially, if not wholly, as untenable as the one overthrown. Nevertheless, the stronger the pressure of economic development, the clearer became its demands and the greater the ability of the revolutionary classes to do what was required of them. The institutions of the revolutionary class which were in opposition to the demands of economic development fell into decay and were soon forgotten. But those which had become necessary quickly struck root and could not be exterminated by the upholders of the former system.

It is in this way that all new social orders have arisen. Revolutionary periods differ from other periods of social development only by virtue of the fact that during them the phenomena of development proceed at an unusually rapid pace.

The genesis of a social institution is, it thus appears, very different from that of a building. Previously perfected plans are not applicable to

the construction of the former. In view of this
fact, sketching plans for the future social state
is about as rational as writing in advance the
history of the next war.

The course of events is, however, by no means
independent of the individual. Everyone who
is active in society affects it to a greater or less
extent. A few individuals, especially prominent
through their capacity or social position, may exercise great influence upon the whole nation.
Some may promote the development of society
by enlightening the people, organizing the revolutionary forces and causing them to act with
vigor and precision; others may retard social development for many years by turning their powers in the opposite direction. The former tend,
by the promotion of the social evolution, to diminish the sufferings and sacrifices that it demands; the latter, on the contrary, tend to increase these sufferings and sacrifices. But no
one, whether he be the mightiest monarch or the
wisest and most benevolent philosopher, can determine at will the direction that the social evolution shall take or prophesy accurately the new
forms that it will adopt.

Few things are, therefore, more childish than
to demand of the socialist that he draw a picture of the commonwealth which he strives for.
This demand, which is made of no other party
than the Socialist Party, is so childish that it
would not deserve much attention were it not
for the fact that it is the objection against socialism which its adversaries raise with soberest
mien.

Never yet in the history of mankind has it happened that a revolutionary party was able to foresee, let alone determine, the forms of the new social order which it strove to usher in. The cause of progress gained much if it could as much as ascertain the tendencies that led to such a new social order, to the end that its political activity could be a conscious, and not merely an instinctive, one. No more can be demanded of the Socialist Party. At the same time, never yet was there a political party that looked so deeply into the social tendencies of its times, and so thoroughly understood them as the Socialist Party.

This is due, not so much to the Socialist Party's merit, as to its good fortune. It owes its superiority to the fact that it stands upon the shoulders of capitalist political economy, the first that ever undertook a scientific investigation of social relations and conditions. One result of this investigation was that the revolutionary classes which overthrew the feudal system of production had a much clearer conception of their social mission and suffered much less from self-deception than any other revolutionary class before them. But the thinkers in the ranks of the Socialist Party have carried the investigations of the social relations much further, they have gone much deeper than any capitalist economist. *Capital,* Karl Marx's great work, has become the lodestar of modern economic science. As far as the work of Karl Marx stands above the works of Quesnay, Adam Smith and Ricardo, just so far stand the socialists of today above the revolutionary classes that appeared at the close of the eighteenth and the beginning of the nineteenth century in point of clearness of vision and certainty of purpose. If the socialists decline to lay before the public a prospectus of the future commonwealth, the bourgeois writers can find in this fact no reason to mock or to conclude that we do not know what we are after. The Socialist Party has a clearer insight into the future than had the path-finders of the present social order.

We have said that a thinker may be able to discover the tendencies of the economic development of his day, but that it is impossible for him to foresee the social forms in which that development will ultimately find expression. A glance at existing conditions will prove the correctness of this view. The tendencies of the capitalist system of production are the same in all countries where it prevails; and yet how different are the political and social forms in England from those in France, those in France from those in Germany, and those in the United States from any of these. Again, the historical tendencies of the labor movement, which has been brought on by the existing system of production, are everywhere identical, and yet we see that the forms under which this movement manifests itself are different in each country.

The tendencies of the capitalist system of production are today well known. Nevertheless, no one would venture to foretell what forms it will take in ten, twenty or thirty years—provided, of course, that it endures that long. And yet some demand of the socialists a detailed description of the social forms that are to come into existence after the present system of production.

It does not follow, however, from the refusal of the socialists to draw up a plan of the future state and the measures which must lead up to it that they consider useless or harmful all thought about the socialist society. The useless and harmful thing is the making of positive propositions for bringing in and organizing the socialist society. Propositions for the shaping of social conditions can be made only where the field is fully under control and well understood. For this reason the Socialist Party can make positive propositions only for the existing social order. Suggestions that go beyond that cannot deal with facts, but must proceed from suppositions; they are, accordingly, phantasies and dreams which remain at best without result. In case their inventor is vigorous and intellectually gifted he may affect the public mind, but the only result will be a waste of time and energy.

We should not, however, confuse with these vagaries those inquiries to ascertain the tendencies that the economic development will or may take as soon as it is transferred from the capitalist to the socialist basis. In such inquiries there is no question of schemes for the future, but of the scientific consideration of results revealed by the investigation of definite facts. Inquiries of this sort are by no means useless; the more clearly we see into the future, the better will we employ our energy in the present. The most noted thinkers of the Socialist Party have undertaken such inquiries. The works of Karl Marx and Frederick Engels contain the results of many investigations of this sort. August Bebel has given in his book on *Woman Under Socialism* the result of his work in this field.

Similar inquiries every thinking socialist has probably carried on in private; for everyone who has placed before himself a great goal realizes the need of clearness in regard to the conditions under which he can reach it. The most widely divergent views have been formed and expressed by persons of different position, temperament, insight into economic questions and acquaintance with other non-capitalistic, especially communistic, forms of society. But such differences in the manner of looking at things in no way disturb the compactness and unity of the Socialist Party. It makes little difference how various may be the views of our goal, so long as our eyes are all turned in the same direction—and that the right one.

We might close this chapter here. But so many false notions about the socialist commonwealth have been inherited from the utopians or invented by ignorant men of letters, that this course would have the appearance of an evasion. Therefore we shall take up certain of then in order to show how the tendencies of our economic development might work themselves out in a socialist community.

7. The "Abolition of the Family."

One of the most widespread prejudices against socialism rests upon the notion that it proposes to abolish the family.

No socialist has the remotest idea of abolishing the family, that is, legally and forcibly dissolving it. Only the grossest misrepresentation can fasten upon socialism any such intention. Moreover, it takes a fool to imagine that a form of family life can be created or abolished by decree.

The modern form of family is in no way opposed to the socialist system of production; the institution of the socialist order, therefore, does not demand the abolition of the family.

What does lead to the abolition of the present form of family life is, not the nature of co-operative production, but economic development. We have already seen in another chapter how under the present system the family is torn to pieces, husband, wife and children are separated, and celibacy and prostitution made common.

The socialist system is not calculated to check economic development; it will, on the contrary, give it a new impulse. This development will continue to draw from the circle of household duties and turn into special industries one occupation after another. That this cannot fail to have in the future, as in the past, its effect on the sphere of woman is self-evident; woman will cease to be a worker in the individual household, and will take her place as a worker in the large industries. But this change will not be to her then, as it is today, a mere transition from household slavery to wage slavery; it will not, as it does today, hurl her from the protection of her home into the most exposed and helpless section of the proletariat. By working side by side with man in the great co-operative industries woman will become his equal and will take an equal part in the community life. She will be his free companion, emancipated not only from the servitude of the house, but also from that of capitalism. Mistress of herself, the equal of man, she will quickly put an end to all prostitution, legal and well as illegal. For the first time in history monogamy will become a real, rather than a fictitious, institution.

These are no utopian suggestions, but scientific conclusions based on definite facts. Whoever wishes to overthrow them must prove the facts non-existent. Since this cannot be done, there remains nothing for the ladies and gentlemen who wish to know nothing of this phase of our development than to become indignant and prove their morality by all manner of lies and misrepresentations. But all their demonstrations will not delay our inevitable evolution a single moment.

This much is certain: whatever alteration the traditional form of the family may undergo, it will not be the act of socialism or of the socialist system of production, but of the economic development that has been going on for the last century. Socialist society cannot retard this development; what it will do is to remove from the economic development all the painful and degrading features that are its inevitable

accompaniments under the capitalist system
production. While, on the one hand, under the
capitalist system of production the economic development is steadily snapping, one after another, the family bonds and destroying family
life, under the socialist system of production,
on the other hand, whatever existing family form
may disappear, can be replaced only by a higher.

8. Confiscation of Property.

Our opponents, who know better than we what
we want and can picture with greater accuracy
the future state, also declare that socialism can
never come into power except through a wholesale confiscation of property, confiscation without
compensation not only of house and farm, but
of superfluous furniture and savings bank deposits. Next to the charge of intending to forcibly dissolve all family ties, this is the trump card
played against us.

The program of the Socialist Party has nothing to say about confiscation. It does not mention it, not from fear of giving offense, but because it is a subject upon which nothing can be
said with certainty. The only thing that can be
declared with certainty is that the tendency of
economic development renders imperative the
social ownership and operation of the means of
large production. In what way this transfer
from private and individual into collective ownership will be effected, whether this inevitable
transfer will take the form of confiscation,
whether it will be a peaceable or a forcible one
—these are questions no man can answer. Past

experience throws little light on this matter. The transition may be effected, as was that from feudalism to capitalism, in as many different ways as there are different countries. The manner of the transition depends wholly upon the general circumstances under which it is effected, the power and enlightenment of the classes concerned, for instance, all of them circumstances that cannot be calculated for the future. In historical development the unexpected plays the most prominent role.

It goes without saying that the Socialist Party wishes this unavoidable expropriation of large industry to be effected with as little friction as possible, in a peaceful way, and with the consent of the whole people. But the historical development will take its course regardless of the wishes of either socialists or their adversaries.

In no case can it be said that the carrying out of the socialist program demands under all circumstances that the property whose expropriation has become necessary, will be confiscated.

Nevertheless, it may be said with certainty that economic development can render necessary the confiscation of only a part of existing property. The economic development demands social ownership of the implements of labor only; it does not concern itself with the part of property that is devoted to personal and private uses. This is applicable not only to food, furniture, etc. We recall what was said in a previous chapter about savings banks. They are the means whereby the private property of the non-capitalist classes is rendered accessible to capitalists.

The deposits of every single depositor, taken separately, are too insignificant to be applied to capitalist industry; not until many deposits have been gathered together are they in a condition to fulfill the function of capital. In the measure in which capitalist undertakings pass from private into social concerns, the opportunities will be lessened for patrons of savings banks to draw interest upon their deposits; these will cease to be capital and will become merely non-interest-bearing funds. But this is a very different thing from the confiscation of savings bank deposits.

The confiscation of such property is, moreover, not only economically unnecessary but politically improbable. These small deposits come mainly from the pockets of the exploited classes, from those classes to whose efforts the introduction of socialism will be due. Only those who consider these classes to be utterly unreliable can believe that they would begin by robbing themselves of their hard-earned savings in order to regain possession of the means of production.

But not only does the introduction of socialist production not require the expropriation of non-productive wealth, it does not even require the expropriation of all property in the means of production.

That which renders the socialist society necessary is large production. Co-operative production requires also co-operative ownership in the means of production. But just as private property in the means of production is irreconcilable with co-operative work in large industry, so co-operative or social ownership in the means of production is irreconcilable with small production. This requires, as we have seen, private ownership in the means of production. The aim of socialism is to place the worker in possession of the necessary means of production. The expropriation of the means of production in small industry would mean merely the senseless proceeding of taking them from their present owner and returning them again to him.

Accordingly, the transition to the socialist society does not at all require the expropriation of the small artisan and the small farmer. This transition not only will deprive them of nothing, but it will bring them many advantages. Since the tendency of socialist society is to substitute production for use for production for sale, it must be its endeavor to transform all social dues (taxes, interest upon mortgages on property that has been nationalized, etc., so far as these may have been not wholly abolished) from money payments into payments in products. But this means the raising of a tremendous burden from the farmer. In many ways that is what he is striving for today, but it is impossible under the supremacy of production for sale. Only the socialist society can bring it, and with it remove the main cause of the ruin of the farming industry.

It is the capitalists who expropriate the farmers and artisans. Socialist society puts an end to this expropriation.

Certainly, socialism will not put an end to economic development. On the contrary, it is the only means to ensure its progress beyond a certain point. In socialist society as in society today large industry will develop more and more and increasingly absorb small industry. But here, too, the same conclusion holds good as in the case of the family and marriage. The direction of the evolution remains the same, but socialism removes all the painful and shocking manifestations that under the present system are the accompaniments of the social evolution.

Today the transformation of the small farmer and the small producer from workers in the field of small production to workers in the field of large production means their transformation from property-holders into proletarians. In a socialist society a farmer or artisan who becomes a worker in a large socialized industry will become a sharer in all the advantages of large industry; his condition is plainly bettered. His transition from large to small industry is no more to be compared with the change from a property-holder to a proletarian, but rather to the transformation of a small property-holder into a large property-holder.

Small production is doomed to disappear. Only the socialist system can make it possible for farmers and handicraftmen to become participants in the advantages of large production without sinking into the proletariat. Only under the socialist system can the inevitable downfall of the small producer, industrial and agricultural, result in an improvement of their condition.

The mainspring of economic development will no longer be the competition which grinds down and expropriates those who fall behind, it will be the power of attraction which the more highly developed forms of production exercise upon the less developed ones.

A development of this sort is not only painless, it proceeds much more rapidly than that brought out by the spur of competition. Today, when the introduction of new and higher forms of production is impossible without ruining and expropriating the owners of industries carried on under inferior forms, and without inflicting suffering and privation upon the large masses of workers who have become through this means superfluous, every economic progress is doggedly resisted. We see on all sides instances of the tenacity with which producers cling to antiquated forms of production, and of their desperate efforts to preserve them. Never yet was any system of production known so revolutionary as the present one; never did any revolutionize so completely within the space of a hundred years all human activities. And yet how many ancient ruins of antiquated, out-lived forms of production still exist!

Just as soon as the fear disappears of being thrown into the proletariat if an independent industry is abandoned; just as soon as the present prejudices against large production disappear because of the advantages which the social ownership of large production will bestow upon all; just as soon as it is possible for everyone to share these advantages, only fools will strive to preserve antiquated forms of production.

What capitalist large production has not accomplished within a hundred years, socialist large production will bring about within a short time, the absorption of outgrown small production. It will accomplish this without expropriation, through the attractive power of improved industrial methods. In places where agricultural production is still not production for sale, but prevailingly production for use, small farming will perhaps continue for some time under the socialist society. In the end the advantages of co-operative large production will be discerned in these districts also. The change from small to large production in agriculture will be hastened and made easy by the steadily progressing disappearance of the contrast between city and country, and by the tendency to locate industries in rural districts.

9. Division of Products in the Future State.

There is still a point, the most important of all, that should be touched upon. The first question which is put to a socialist is usually: How will you go about the division of wealth? Shall each have an equal share?

"Dividing up!" That sticks in the crop of the Philistine. Their whole conception of socialism begins and ends with that word. Indeed, even among the cultured the idea prevails that the object of socialism is to divide the whole wealth of the nation among the people.

That this view still prevails, despite all protests and proofs on the part of socialists, is to be ascribed not only to the malice of our opponents, but also, and perhaps to a greater extent, to their inability to understand the social conditions that have been created by the development of large production. Their horizon is still, to a great extent, bounded by the conceptions that belong only to small production. From the standpoint of small production "dividing up" is the only possible form of socialism. The notion of dividing has long been familiar to the small business man and farmer. From the beginning of production for sale in antiquity, it has happened innumerable times that as soon as a few families had heaped up great wealth and reduced farmers and artisans to a state of dependence, these latter rose in rebellion and attempted to improve their condition through the expulsion of the rich and the division of their property. They succeeded in this for the first time during the French Revolution, which laid such stress on the rights of private property. Peasants, artisans and the class that was about to develop into capitalists, divided among themselves the church estates. "Dividing up" is the socialism of small production, the socialism of the conservative ranks of society, not the socialism of the proletariat engaged in large industry.

Socialists do not propose to divide: on the contrary, their object is to concentrate in the hands of society the instruments of production that are now scattered in the hands of various owners.

But this does not dispose of the question of "dividing up." If the means of production belong to society, to it must belong also, as a matter of course, the function of disposing of the prod-acts that are brought forth by the use of these means. In what way will society distribute these among its members? Shall it be according to the principle of equality or according to the labor performed by each? And in the latter case, is every kind of labor to receive the same reward, whether it be pleasant or unpleasant, hard or easy, skilled or unskilled?

The answer to this question seems to be the central point of socialism. Not only does it greatly preoccupy the opponents of socialism, but even the early socialists devoted a great deal of attention to it. From Fourier to Weitling and from Weitling to Bellamy, there runs a steady stream of the most diversified answers, many of which reveal a wonderful cleverness. There is no lack of positive propositions, many of which are as simple as they are practicable. Nevertheless, the question has not the importance generally ascribed to it.

There was a time when the distribution of products was looked upon as wholly independent of production. Since the contradictions and ills of the capitalist system manifest themselves first in its peculiar method of distributing its products, it was quite natural that the exploited classes and their friends should have found the root of all evil in the "unjust" distribution of products. Of course, they proceeded, in accordance with the ideas prevalent at the beginning of the nineteenth century, upon the supposition that the existing system of distribution was the result of the ideas of the day, especially of the legal system in force. In order to remove this unjust distribution, all that was needed was to invent a juster one, and to convince the world of its advantages. The just system could be no other than the reverse of the existing one. "Today the grossest inequality rules; the principle upon which distribution should be based must be one of equality." Today the idler rolls in wealth while the laborer starves, so others said: "To each according to his deeds" (or in newer form, "To each the product of his labor"). But doubts arose as to both these formulas, and so arose a third: "To each according to his needs."

Since then socialists have come to realize that the distribution of products in a community is determined, not by the prevailing legal system, but by the prevailing system of production. The share of the landlord, the capitalist and the wage-earner in the total product of society is determined by the part which land, capital and labor-power play in the present system of production. Certainly in a socialist society the distribution of products will not be left to the working of blind laws concerning the operation of which those concerned are unconscious. As today in a large industrial establishment production and the payment of wages are carefully regulated, so in a socialist society, which is nothing more than a single gigantic industrial concern, the same principle must prevail. The rules according to which the distribution of products is to be carried out will be established by those concerned. Nevertheless, it will not depend upon their pleasure what these rules shall be; they will not be adopted arbitrarily according to this or that "principle," they will be determined by the actual conditions of society and, above all, by the conditions of production.

For instance, the degree of productivity of labor, at any given time, exercises a great influence upon the manner in which distribution is effected. We can conceive a time when science shall have raised industry to such a high level of productivity that everything wanted by man will be produced in great abundance. In such a case, the formula, "To each according to his needs," would be applied as a matter of course and without difficulty. On the other hand, not even the profoundest conviction of the justice of this formula would be able to put it into practice if the productivity of labor remained so low that the proceeds of the most excessive toil could produce only the bare necessities. Again, the formula, "To each according to his deeds," will always be found inapplicable. If it has any meaning at all, it presupposes a distribution of the total product of the commonwealth among its members. This notion, like that of a general division with which the socialist regime is to be ushered in, springs from the modes of thought that are peculiar to the modern system of private property. To distribute all products at stated intervals would be equivalent to the gradual reintroduction of private property in the means of production.

The very principle of socialist production limits the possible distribution to only a portion of the products. All those products which are requisite to the enlargement of production cannot, as a matter of course, be the subject of distribution; and the same holds good with regard to all such products as are intended for common use, *i. e.,* for the establishment, preservation or enlargement of public institutions.

Already in modern society the number and size of such institutions increases steadily. It is in this domain especially that large production crowds down small production. It goes without saying that so far from being checked, this development will be greatly stimulated in a socialist society.

The quantity of products that can be absorbed by private consumption and, accordingly, be turned into private property, must inevitably be a much smaller portion of the total product in a socialist, than in modern, society, where almost all the products are merchandise and private property. In socialist society it is not the bulk of the products, but only the residue, that is distributed.

But even this residue socialist society will not be able to dispose of at will; there, too, the requirements of production will determine the course to be pursued. Such production is undergoing steady changes; the forms and methods of distribution will be subject to manifold changes in a socialist society.

It is entirely utopian to imagine that a special system of distribution is to be manufactured, and that it will stand for all time. In this matter, as little as any other, is socialist society likely to move by leaps and bounds, or start all over anew; it will go on from the point at which capitalist society ceases. The distribution of goods in a socialist society might possibly continue for some time under forms that are essentially developments of the existing system of wage-payment. At any rate, this is the point from which it is bound to start. Just as the forms of wage-labor differ today, not only from time to time, but also in various branches of industry, and in various sections of the country, so also may it happen that in a socialist society the distribution of products may be carried on under a variety of forms corresponding to the various needs of the population and the historical antecedents of the industry. We must not think of the socialist society as something rigid and uniform, but rather as an organism, constantly developing, rich in possibilities of change, an organism that is to develop naturally from increasing division of labor, commercial exchange, and the dominance of society by science and art.

Next to the thought of "dividing up," that of "equal shares" troubles the foes of socialism most. "Socialism," they declare, "proposes that everyone shall have an equal share of the total product; the industrious is to have no more than the lazy; hard and disagreeable labor is to receive no higher reward than that which is light and agreeable; the hod-carrier who has nothing to do but carry the material is to be on a par with the architect himself. Under such circumstances everyone will work as little as possible; no one will perform the hard and disagreeable tasks; knowledge, having ceased to be appreciated, will cease to be cultivated; and the final

result will be the relapse of society into barbarism. Consequently, socialism is impracticable."

The fallacy of this reasoning is too glaring to
need exposure. This much may be said: Should
socialist society ever decide to decree equality of
incomes, and should the effect of such a measure
threaten to be the dire one prophesied, the natural
result would be, not that socialist production, but
that the principle of equality of incomes, would
be thrown overboard.

The foes of socialism would be justified in
concluding from the equality of incomes that
socialism is impracticable if they could prove:

(1) That this equality would be under all
circumstances irreconcilable with the progress of
production. This they never have, and never
can, prove, because the activity of the individual
in production does not depend solely upon his
remuneration, but upon a great variety of circumstances—his sense of duty, his ambition, his
dignity, his pride, etc.—none of which can be
the subject of positive prophecy, but only of conjecture, a conjecture which makes against, and
not for, the opinion expressed by the opponents
of socialism.

(2) That the equality of incomes is so essential to a socialist society that the latter cannot
be conceived without the former. The opponents of socialism will find it equally impossible
to prove this. A glance over the various forms
of communist production from the primitive
communism down to the latest communist societies will reveal how manifold are the forms of
distribution that are applicable to a community

of property in the instruments of production. All forms of modern wage-payment-fixed salaries, piece wages, time wages, bonuses—all of them are reconcilable with the spirit of a socialist society; and there is not one of them that may not play a role in socialist society, as the wants and customs of its members, together with the requirements of production, may demand.

It does not, however, follow from this that the principle of equality of incomes—not necessarily identical with their uniformity—will play no part in socialist society. What is certain is that it will do so not as the aim of a movement for leveling things generally, forcibly, artificially, but as the result of a natural development, a social tendency.

In the capitalist system of production there exist two tendencies, one to increase and the other to decrease the differences in incomes; one to increase, one to diminish inequality. By dissolving the middle classes of society and swelling constantly the size of individual fortunes the capitalist system broadens and deepens the chasm that exists between the masses of the population and those who are at its head, the latter tower higher and higher above the former. Together with this tendency, is noticed another, which, operating within the circle of the masses themselves, steadily equalizes their incomes. It flings the small producers, farmers and manufacturers, into the class of the proletariat, or at least, pushes their incomes down to the proletarian level, and wipes out existing differences among the proletarians themselves. The machine tends steadily to remove all differences which originally appeared in the proletariat. Today the differences in wages among the various strata of labor fluctuate incessantly and come nearer and nearer to a point of uniformity. At the same time, the incomes of the educated proletariat are irresistibly tending downward. The equalization of incomes among the masses—that which the opponents of socialism, with the greatest moral indignation, brand as the purpose of socialism—is going on before their eyes in the society of today.

Under the socialist system, as a matter of course, all those tendencies that sharpen inequalities and that proceed from private ownership in the means of production, would come to an end. On the other hand, the tendency to wipe out inequalities of incomes would find stronger expression. But here, again, the observations made upon the dissolution of existing family forms and the downfall of small production hold good. The tendency of economic development remains in socialist, as in capitalist, society, but it finds a very different expression. Today the equalization of incomes among the mass of the population proceeds by the depression of the higher incomes to the level of the lower ones. In a socialist society it must inevitably proceed by the raising of the lower to the standard of the higher.

The opponents of socialism seek to frighten the small producers and the working-men with the claim that equalization of incomes can mean for them nothing else than a lowering of their condition, because, they say, the incomes of the wealthy classes are not sufficient, if divided among the poor, to preserve the present average income of the working and middle classes; consequently, if there is to be an equality of incomes, the upper classes of workers and the small producers will have to give up part of their incomes, and will thus be the losers under socialism.

Whatever truth there may be in this claim lies in the fact that the wretchedly poor, especially the slum proletariat, are today so numerous and their need so great that to divide among them the immense incomes of the rich would scarcely be enough to make possible for them the existence of a worker of the better-paid class. Whether this is a sufficient reason for preserving our glorious social system may very well be doubted. We are of the opinion, however, that a diminution of the misery, which would be accomplished through such a division, would mean a step forward.

There is, however, no question of "dividing up"; the only question is concerning a change in the method of production. The transformation of the capitalist system of production into the socialist system of production must inevitably result in a rapid increase of the quantity of wealth produced. It must never be lost sight of that the capitalist system of production for sale hinders today the progress of economic development, hinders the full expansion of the productive forces that lie latent in society. Not only is it unable to absorb the small industries as rapidly as the technical development makes possible and desirable, but it has even become impossible for it to employ all the labor forces that are available. The capitalist system of production squanders these forces; it steadily drives increasing numbers of workers into the ranks of the unemployed, the slum proletariat, the parasites and the unproductive middlemen.

Such a state of things would be impossible in a socialist society. It could not fail to find productive labor for all its available labor forces. It would increase, it might even double, the number of productive workers; in the measure in which it did this it would multiply the total wealth produced yearly. This increase in production would be enough in itself to raise the incomes of all workers, not only of the poorest.

Furthermore, since socialist production would promote the absorption of small production by large production and thus increase the productivity of labor, it would be possible, not only to raise the incomes of the workers, but also to shorten the hours of labor.

In view of this, it is foolish to claim that socialism means the equality of pauperism. This is not the equality of socialism; it is the equality of the modern system of production. Socialist production must inevitably improve the condition of all the working classes, including the small industrialist and the small farmer. According to the economic conditions under which the change from capitalism to socialism is effected this improvement will be greater or less, but in any case it will be marked. And every economic advance beyond that will produce an increase, and not, as today, a decrease, in the general well-being.

This change in the tendency of incomes is, in the eyes of socialists, of much more importance than the absolute increase of incomes. The thoughtful man lives more in the future than in the present; what the future threatens or promises preoccupies him more than the enjoyment of the present. Not what is, but what will be, not existing conditions, but tendencies, determine the happiness both of individuals and of whole states.

Thus we become acquainted with another element of superiority in socialist over capitalist society. It affords, not only a greater well-being, but also certainty of livelihood—a security that today the greatest fortune cannot guarantee. If greater well-being affects only those who have hitherto been exploited, security of livelihood is a boon to the present exploiters, whose well-being demands no improvement or is capable of none. Uncertainty hovers over both rich and poor, and it is, perhaps, more trying than want itself. In imagination it forces those to taste the bitterness of want who are not yet subject to it; it is a specter that haunts the palaces of the wealthiest.

All observers who have become acquainted with communist societies, whether they were situated in India, France or America, have been struck with the appearance of calmness, confidence and equanimity peculiar to their members. Independent of the oscillations of the market, and in possession of their own instruments of production, they are self-sufficient; they regulate their labor in accordance with their needs, and they know in advance just what they have to expect. And yet the security enjoyed by these communities is far from being perfect. Their control over nature is slight, the societies themselves are small. Mishaps brought on by diseases of cattle, failures of crops, freshets, etc., are frequent and smite the whole body. Upon how much firmer a basis would a socialist community stand with boundaries co-extensive with those of a nation and with all the conquests of science at its command!

10. Socialism and Freedom.

That a socialist society would afford its members comfort and security has been admitted even by many of the opponents of socialism. "But" they say, "these advantages are bought at too dear a price; they are paid for with a total loss of freedom. The bird in a cage may have sufficient daily food; it also is secure against hunger and the inclemencies of the weather. But it has lost its freedom, and for that reason is a pitiful thing. It yearns for a chance to take its place among the dangers of the outside world, to struggle for its own existence." They maintain that socialism destroys economic freedom, the freedom of labor; that it introduces a despotism in comparison with which the most unrestricted absolutism would be freedom.

So great is the fear of this slavery that even some socialists have been seized with it, and have become anarchists. They have as great a horror of communism as of production for sale, and they attempt to escape both by seeking both. They want to have communism and production for sale together. Theoretically, this is absurd; in practice, it could amount to nothing more than the establishment of voluntary co-operative societies for mutual aid.

It is true that socialist production is irreconcilable with the full freedom of labor, that is, with the freedom of the laborer to work when, where and how he wills. But this freedom of the laborer is irreconcilable with any systematic, co-operative form of labor, whether the form be capitalist or socialist. Freedom of labor is possible only in small production, and even there only up to a certain point. Even where small production is freed from all restrictive regulations, the individual worker still remains a dependent on natural or social conditions; the farmer, for example, on the weather, the artisan on the state of the market. Nevertheless, small production offers the possibility of a certain degree of freedom; this is its ideal, the most revolutionary ideal of which the small bourgeois is capable. A hundred years ago at the time of the French Revolution this ideal was based on industrial conditions. Today it has no economic basis and can persist only in the heads of people who are unable to perceive that an economic revolution has taken place. It is not the socialist who destroy this "freedom of labor," but the resistless progress of large production. The very ones from whom is heard most frequently the declaration that labor must be free are the capitalists, those who have contributed most to overthrow that freedom.

Freedom of labor has come to an end, not only in the factory, but wherever the individual worker is only a link in a long chain of workers. It does not exist either for the manual worker or for the brain worker employed in any industry. The hospital physician, the school teacher, the railroad employe, the newspaper writer— none of these enjoy the freedom of labor; they are all bound to certain rules, they must all be at their post at a certain hour.

It is true that in one respect the workingman does enjoy freedom under the capitalist system. If the work does not suit him in one factory, he is free to seek work in another; he can change his employer. In a socialist community, where all the means of production are in a single hand, there is but one employer; to change is impossible.

In this respect the wage-earner today has a certain freedom in comparison with the worker in a socialist society, but this cannot be called a freedom of labor. However frequently a worker may change his place of work today, he will not find freedom. In each place the activities of every individual worker are defined and regulated. This has become a technical necessity.

Accordingly, the freedom with the loss of which the worker is threatened in a socialist society is not freedom of labor, but freedom to choose his master. Under the present system

this freedom is of no slight importance; it is a
protection to the workingman. But even this
freedom is gradually destroyed by the progress
of capitalism. The increasing number of the
unemployed reduces constantly the number of
positions that are open and throws upon the
labor market more applicants than there are
places. The idle workingman is, as a rule, happy
if he can secure work of any sort. Furthermore,
the increased concentration of the means of production in a few hands has a steady tendency to
place over the workingman the same employer
or set of employers whichever way he may turn.
Inquiry, therefore, shows that what is decried
as the wicked and tyrannical purpose of socialism is but the natural tendency of the economic
development of modern society.

Socialism will not, and cannot, check this development; but in this as in so many other respects socialism can obviate the evils that accompany the development. It cannot remove the
dependence of the working-man upon the mechanism of production in which he is one of the
wheels; but it substitutes for the dependence of
a working-man upon a capitalist with interests
hostile to him a dependence upon a society of
which he is himself a member, a society of equal
comrades, all of whom have the same interests.

It can be easily understood why a liberal-
minded lawyer or author may consider such a
dependence unbearable, but it is not unbearable
to the modern proletarian, as a glance at the
trade union movement will show. The organizations of labor furnish a picture of the "tyr-

anny of the socialist paternal state" of which the opponents of socialism have so much to say. In the organizations of labor the rules under which each member is to work are laid down minutely and enforced strictly. Yet it has never occurred to any member of such an organization that these rules were an unbearable restriction upon his personal liberty. Those who have found it incumbent upon them to defend the freedom of labor against this "terrorism," and who have done so often with force of arms and bloodshed, were never the working-men, but their exploiters. Poor Freedom! which has today no defenders except slaveholders!

But in a socialist community the lack of freedom in work would not only lose its oppressive character, it would also become the foundation of the highest freedom yet possible to man. This seems a contradiction, but the contradiction is only apparent.

Down to the day when large production began, the labor employed in the production of the necessities of life took up the whole time of those engaged in it; it required the fullest exercise of both body and mind. This was true, not only of the fisherman and the hunter, but also of the farmer, the mechanic and the merchant. The existence of the human being engaged in production was consumed almost wholly by his occupation. It was labor that steeled his sinews and nerves, that quickened his brain and made him anxious to acquire knowledge. But the further division of labor was carried, the more one-sided did it make the producers. Mind and body ceased to exercise themselves in a variety of directions and to develop all their powers. Wholly taken up by incomplete momentary tasks, the producers lost the capacity to comprehend phenomena as organic wholes. A harmonious, well-rounded development of physical and mental powers, a deep concern in the problems of nature and society, a philosophical bent of mind, that is, a searching for the highest truth for its own sake,—none of these could be found under such circumstances, except among those classes who remained free from the necessity of toil. Until the commencement of the era of machinery this was possible only by throwing upon others the burden of labor, by exploiting them. The most ideal, the most philosophic race that history has yet known, the only society of thinkers and artists devoted to science and art for their own sakes, was the Athenian aristocracy, the slaveholding landlords of Athens.

Among them all labor, whether slave or free, was regarded as degrading—and justly so. It was no presumption on the part of Socrates when he said: "Traders and mechanics lack culture. They have no leisure, and without leisure no good education is possible. They learn only what their trade requires of them; knowledge in itself has no attraction for them. They take up arithmetic only for the sake of trade, not for the purpose of acquiring a knowledge of numbers. It is not given to them to strive for higher things. The merchant and mechanic say: 'The pleasure derived from honor and knowledge is of no value when compared with money-making.' However skilled smiths, carpenters and shoemakers may be at their trade, most of them are animated only by the souls of slaves; they know not the true nor the beautiful."

Economic development has advanced since those days. The division of labor has reached a point undreamt of, and the system of production for sale has driven many of the former exploiters and people of culture into the class of producers. Like the mechanics and farmers, the rich also are wholly taken up with their business. They do not now assemble in gymnasiums and academies, but in stock exchanges and markets. The speculations in which they are absorbed do not concern questions of truth and justice, but the prices of wool and whiskey, bonds and coupons. These are the speculations that consume their mental energies. After this "labor" they have neither strength nor taste for any but the most commonplace amusements.

On the other hand, as far as the cultured classes are concerned, their education has become a merchandise. They, too, have neither time nor inclination for disinterested search for truth, for striving after the ideal. Each buries himself in his specialty and considers every moment lost which is spent in learning anything which cannot be turned into money. Hence the movement to abolish Greek and Latin from the secondary schools. Whatever the pedagogic grounds may be for this movement, the real reason is the desire to have the youth taught only what is "useful," that is, what can be turned into money. Even among scientific men and artists the instinct after a harmonious development is perceptibly losing ground. On all sides specialists are springing up. Science and art are degraded to the level of a trade. What Socrates said of ancient handicraft now holds good of these pursuits. The philosophic way of looking at things is on the decline—that is, within the classes here considered.

In the meantime, a new sort of labor has sprung up—machine labor; and a new class—the proletariat.

The machine robs labor of all intellectual activity. The working-man at a machine no longer needs to think; all that he has to do is silently to obey the machine. The machine dictates to him what he has to do; he has become an appendage to it. What is said of hand labor applies also, though to a slighter extent, to home-work and hand-work done in the factory. The division of labor in the production of a single article among innumerable working-men paves the way for the introduction of machinery.

The first result of the monotony and absence of intellectual activity in the work of the proletarian is the apparent dulling of his mind.

The second result is that he is driven to revolt against excessive hours of work. To him labor is not identical with life; life commences only when labor is at an end. For working-men to whom labor and life were identical, freedom of labor meant freedom of life. The working-man, who lives only when he does not work, can enjoy a free life only by being free from labor. As a matter of course, the efforts of this class of workers cannot be directed to freeing themselves from all labor. Labor is the condition of life. But their efforts will necessarily be directed toward reducing their hours of labor far enough to leave them time to live.

This is one of the principal causes of the struggle on the part of the modern proletariat to shorten the hours of work, a struggle which would have had no meaning to the farmers and mechanics of former social systems. The struggle of the proletariat for shorter hours is not aimed at economic advantages, such as a rise in wages or the reduction of the number of unemployed. The struggle for shorter hours is a *struggle for life*.

But the unintellectual character of machine work has a third result. The intellectual powers of the proletariat are not exhausted by their labor as are those of other workers; they lie fallow during work. For this reason the craving of the proletarian to exercise his mind outside of his hours of work is just so much the stronger. One of the most remarkable phenomena in modern society is the thirst for knowledge displayed by the proletariat. While all other classes kill their time with the most unintellectual diversions, the proletarian displays a passion for intellectual culture. Only one who has had an opportunity to associate with the proletariat can fully realize the strength of this thirst after knowledge and enlightenment. But even the outsider may imagine it, if he compares the newspapers, magazines and pamphlets of the workers with the literature that finds acceptance in other social circles.

And this thirst for knowledge is entirely disinterested. Knowledge cannot help the worker at a machine to increase his income. He seeks truth for its own sake, not for material profit. Accordingly, he does not limit himself to any one domain of knowledge; he tries to embrace the whole; he seeks to understand the whole of society, the whole world. The most difficult problems attract him most; it is often hard to bring him down from the clouds to solid earth.

It is not the possesison of knowledge but the effort to acquire it that makes the philosopher. It is among the despised and ignorant proletariat that the philosophical spirit of the brilliant members of the Athenian aristocracy is revived. But the free development of this spirit is not possible in modern society. The proletariat is without means to instruct itself; it is deprived of opportunities for systematic study, it is exposed to all the dangers and inconveniences of planless self-instruction; above all, it lacks sufficient leisure. Science and art remain to the proletariat a promised land which it looks at from a distance, which it struggles to possess, but which it cannot enter.

Only the triumph of Socialism can render accessible to the proletariat all the sources of culture. Only the triumph of socialism can make possible the reduction of the hours of work to such a point that the working-man can enjoy leisure enough to acquire adequate knowledge. The capitalist system of production wakens the proletarian's desire for knowledge; the socialist system alone can satisfy it.

It is not the freedom of labor, but the *freedom from labor,* which in a socialist society the use of machinery makes increasingly possible, that will bring to mankind freedom of life, freedom for artistic and intellectual activity, freedom for the noblest enjoyment.

That blessed, harmonious culture, which has only once appeared in the history of mankind and was then the privilege of a small body of select aristocrats, will become the common property of all civilized nations. What slaves were to the ancient Athenians, machinery will be to modern man. Man will feel all the elevating influences that flow from freedom from productive toil, without being poisoned by the evil influences which, through chattel slavery, finally undermined the Athenian aristocracy. And as the modern means of science and art are vastly superior to those of two thousand years ago, and the civilization of today overshadows that of the little land of Greece, so will the socialist commonwealth outshine in moral greatness and material well-being the most glorious society that history has thus far known.

Happy the man to whom it is given to contribute his strength to the realization of this ideal.

V. THE CLASS STRUGGLE.

1. Socialism and the Property-Holding Classes.

The last paragraphs of our declaration of principles reads as follows: "This social transformation means the liberation, not only of the proletariat, but of the whole human race. Only the working-class, however, can bring it about. All other classes, despite their conflicting interests, maintain their existence on the basis of the private ownership of the means of production, and therefore have a common motive for supporting the principles of the existing social order.

"The struggle of the working-class against capitalist exploitation is necessarily a political struggle. The working-class cannot develop its economic organization and wage its economic battles without political rights. It cannot accomplish the transfer of the means of production to the community as a whole without first having come into possession of political power.

"To make this struggle of the workers conscious and unified, to keep its one great object in view,—this is the purpose of the Socialist Party."

In all lands where capitalist production prevails the interests of the working-class are identical. With the development of world-commerce and production for the world-market the position of the workers in each country becomes increasingly dependent on that of the workers in other countries. The liberation of the working-class is, therefore, a task in which the workers of all civilized lands are equally concerned. Being conscious of this fact the Socialist Party proclaims its solidarity with the class-conscious workers of all lands.

"The Socialist Party, accordingly, struggles, not for any class privileges, but for the abolition of classes and class-rule, for equal rights and equal duties for all, without distinction of sex or race. In conformity with these principles it opposes in present day society, not only the exploitation and oppression of wage-workers, but also every form of exploitation and oppression, be it directed against a class, a party, a sex, or a race."

The introductory sentence of the first of these paragraphs needs little explanation. We have already shown that the triumph of socialism is in the interest of our entire social development. In a certain sense it is even in the interest of the owning and exploiting classes. These, like their victims, suffer from the contradictions of the modern method of production. Some of them degenerate in idleness, others wear themselves out in the ceaseless race for profits; while over them all hangs the Damocles' sword of bank-ruptcy.

But observation teaches us that the great majority of the owners and exploiters are bitterly opposed to socialism. Can this be due simply to lack of knowledge and insight? The spokesmen among the adversaries of socialism are, on the contrary, the very persons whose positions in the government, in society, and in science should fit

them best of all to understand the social mechanism and to perceive the law of social evolution.

And so shocking are the conditions in modern
society that no one who wishes to be taken se-
riously in politics or science dares any longer
to deny the truth of the charges preferred by
socialism against the present social order. On
the contrary the clearest thinkers in all the capitalist political parties admit that there is "some
truth" in those charges; some even declare that
the final triumph of socialism is inevitable unless
society suddenly turns about and reforms—a
thing these gentlemen imagine can be done offhand, provided the demands of this or that party
be promptly granted. In this manner even those
among the non-socialist parties who best understand the socialist critique of capitalist society
save themselves from accepting the conclusions
of this critique.

The cause of this remarkable phenomenon is
not difficult to discover. Although certain important interests of the property-holding classes
plead against the private ownership of the means
of production, other interests, more immediate
and easily discernible, demand its retention.

This is especially the case with the rich. They
can expect no immediate gain from the abolition
of private property in the means of production.
The beneficent results that would flow therefrom
would be ultimately felt by them as well as by
society in general, but such results are comparatively distant. The disadvantages which they
would suffer are, on the other hand, self-evident;
the power and distinction they enjoy today would

disappear at once, and not a few might be deprived, also, of their present ease and comfort.

It is otherwise with the lower ranks of the property-holding classes, the small producers, merchants and farmers. These have nothing to lose in point of power and distinction, and they can only gain in point of ease and comfort by the introduction of the socialist system of production. But in order to realize this they must rise above the point of view of their own class. From the standpoint of these small capitalists or farmers the capitalist system of production is unintelligible; modern socialism, naturally, they can understand still less. The one thing they have a clear notion of is the necessity of private ownership in their own implements of labor if their system of production is to be preserved. So long as the small manufacturer reasons as a small manufacturer, the small farmer as a small farmer, the small merchant as a small merchant, so long as they are still possessed of a strong sense of their own class, so long will they be bound to the idea of private ownership in the means of production, so long will they instinctively resist socialism, however ill they may fare under capitalism.

We have seen in a previous chapter how private property in the means of production fetters the small producers to their undeveloped occupations long after these have ceased to afford them a competence, and even when they might improve their condition by becoming wage-workers outright. Thus private ownership in the means of production is the force that binds all the property-holding classes to the capitalist system, even those who are themselves among the exploited, whose property-holding has become a bitter mockery.

Only those individuals among the small capitalists and farmers who have despaired of the preservation of their class, who are no longer blind to the fact that the form of production upon which they depend for a living is doomed, are in a position to understand the principles of socialism. But lack of information and narrowness of view, both of which are natural results of their condition, make it difficult for them to realize the utter hopelessness of their class. Their misery and their hysterical search for a means of salvation have hitherto only had the effect of making them the easy prey of any demagog who was sufficiently self-assertive and who did not stick at promises.

Among the upper ranks of the property-holding classes there exists a higher degree of culture and a broader view. Here and there a few individuals are still affected by idealistic reminiscences from the days of the early revolutionary struggles. But woe to the person in these upper ranks who shows an interest in socialism or engages in its propaganda! He must soon choose between giving up his ideas or breaking all the social bonds that have held and supported him. Few possess the vigor and independence of character requisite to approach the point where the roads fork; few among these few are brave enough to break with their own class when they have reached the point; and, finally, of these few

among the few the greater portion have hitherto
soon grown tired, recognized the "indiscretions
of their youth," and finally turned "sensible."

The idealists among the upper classes are the
only ones whose support it is at all possible to en-
list in favor of socialism. But even among these
the majority are moved by the insight which
they have acquired only far enough to wear
themselves out in fruitless searchings for a
peaceful solution of the social problem; that is
to say, in searching for a solution that will recon-
cile the interests of the capitalist class with their
more or less developed knowledge of socialism
and their consciences.

Only those bourgeois idealists develop into
genuine socialists who have, not only the requisite theoretical insight, but also the courage and
strength to break with their class.

Accordingly, the cause of socialism has little
to hope from the property-holding classes. Individual members may be won over to socialism,
but only such as no longer belong by convictions
and conduct to the class to which their economic
position assigns them. These will ever be a
very small minority, except when, during revolutionary periods, the scales incline to the side
of socialism. Only at such times may the socialists look forward to a stampede from the
ranks of the property-holding classes.

Thus far the only favorable recruiting ground
for the socialist army has been, not the classes
which still have something to lose, however little
that may be, but the class of those who have
nothing to lose but their chains, and a world to
gain.

2. Servants and Menials.

The recruiting ground of socialism is the class of the propertyless, but not all ranks of this class are equally favorable.

Though it is false to say, with the Philistines, that there have always been poor people, it is nevertheless true that pauperism is as old as the system of production for sale. At first it appeared only as an exceptional phenomenon. In the Middle Ages, for example, there were but few who did not own the instruments of production necessary for the satisfaction of their own wants. In those days it was an easy matter for the comparatively small number of propertyless persons to find situations with the property-holding families as assistants, farm-hands, journeymen, maids, etc. These were generally young persons, and their lot was alleviated by the prospect of establishing their own workshops and owning their own homes. In all cases they worked with the head of the family or his wife, and enjoyed in common with them the fruits of their labor. As members of a property-holding family they were not proletarians; they felt an interest in the property of the family whose prosperity and adversity they shared alike. Where servants are part of the family of the property-holder, they will be found ready to defend property even though they have none themselves. Among such socialism cannot strike root.

The position of the apprentices was much the same as that of the classes just discussed (Compare Ch. II., i.).

Gradually, however, there grew up beside these classes, which really took part in production, another class, that of personal servants. Some of the poor turned for support to the families of the greater exploiters. In the Middle Ages this meant entering the personal service of the nobles, rich merchants, or higher clergy. The poor entered this service, not to assist in productive labor, but to act as mercenary soldiers or mere lackeys. The ancient feeling of mutual interest has disappeared, but a new one has taken its place. There are various grades of servants, with different work and different pay. Each individual is eager to improve his position by any means within his power. His success is dependent on the master's favor. The more skillfully he adapts himself, the better are his prospects. Again, the larger the income of the master and the greater his power and distinction, the more plentiful are the crumbs which fall to his menials; this holds especially of those menials who are kept for show, whose only task is to make a parade of the superfluities which their master enjoys, to assist him in squandering his wealth, and to stand by him loyally if he commits crime or folly. The modern servant, accordingly, comes into relations of peculiar intimacy with his master, and thus he has naturally developed into a foe of the oppressed and exploited working-class; not infrequently he is more ruthless than his master in his treatment of them. The master, if he has any discretion at all, will not kill the hen that lays the golden egg; he will preserve her, not only for himself, but also for his successors. The menial is not restrained by any such considerations.

Small wonder that among the people generally nothing is more hated than this class of menials. Their subservience toward those above and their brutality toward those below have become proverbial.

The characteristics of the menial are, however, not confined to the propertyless people of the lower classes. The poverty-stricken noble seeking a livelihood as courtier is on a level with the servant of the lowest class.

But we are here dealing with menials of this latter class. The growing intensity of exploitation, the constantly swelling surplus enjoyed by the capitalist, together with his resulting extravagance, all favor a steady increase in the number of those employed as servants. That is to say, they favor the growth of a class which, despite its lack of property, is not at all a promising recruiting ground for the socialist movement.

But other tendencies, fortunately, are working in the opposite direction. The steady revolution in industry, with its encroachments upon the family, its withdrawal of one occupation after another from the sphere of household duties and the assignment of them to special industries, and, above all, the infinite division and subdivision of labor, are building up the various trades of barbers, waiters, cab drivers, etc. Long after these and similar trades have lost their domestic character they tend to preserve the characteristics of their origin; nevertheless, as time passes, these characteristics wear off, and the members of these trades acquire the qualities of the industrial wage-working class.

3. The Slums.

However numerous the class of menials may be, it has not, as a rule, been able to absorb the whole number of those left propertyless. The unemployable, children, old people, sick and cripples have been from the beginning unable to earn a living by entering into service. To these were added at the beginning of modern times a large number who could work but found nothing to do. For them there was nothing but to beg, steal, or prostitute themselves. They were compelled either to perish or to throw overboard all sense of shame, honor and self-respect. They prolong their existence only by giving precedence to their immediate wants over their regard for their reputations. That such a condition cannot but exercise the most demoralizing and corrupting influence is self-evident.

Furthermore, the effect of this influence is intensified by the fact that the unemployed poor are utterly superfluous to the existing order; their extinction would relieve it of an undesirable burden. A class that has become superfluous, that has no necessary function to fulfil, must degenerate.

And beggars cannot even raise themselves in their own estimation by indulging in the self-deception that they are necessary to the social system; they have no recollection of a time when their class performed any useful services; they have no way of forcing society to support them as parasites. They are only tolerated. Humility is, consequently, the first duty of the beggar and the highest virtue of the poor. Like the menials, this class of the proletariat is servile toward the powerful; it furnishes no opposition to the existing social order. On the contrary, it ekes out its existence from the crumbs that fall from the tables of the rich. Why should it wish to abolish its benefactors? Furthermore, beggars are not themselves exploited; the higher the degree of exploitation, the larger the incomes of the rich, all the more have the beggars to expect. Like the menial class, they are partakers in the fruits of exploitation; they have no motive for wishing to put an end to the system.

But though this section of the proletariat has never offered any resistance to the system of exploitation, still it cannot be regarded as a bulwark of this system. Cowardly and unprincipled, it soon deserts its benefactors when power and wealth have slipped from their hands. This class has never taken the lead in any revolutionary movement. But it has always been on hand during social disturbances, ready to fish in troubled waters. Occasionally it has given the last kick to a falling class; as a rule, however, it has satisfied itself with exploiting every revolution that has broken out, only to betray it at the earliest opportunity.

The capitalist system of production has greatly increased the slum proletariat. It constantly sends to it new recruits. In the large centers of industry this element constitutes a considerable portion of the population.

In character and view of life the slum proletariat approaches the lowest ranks of the farmer and small bourgeois class. Like these, it has despaired of its own power and seeks to save itself through aid received from above.

4. The Beginnings of the Wage-Earning Proletariat.

It was from the last mentioned classes that capitalism drew its first supply of wage-labor. It needed not so much skilled workers as docile ones. And since the slum-proletariat and the sections of the population most closely related to it had already learned obedience and humility they were well fitted to supply the demand. With workers from this source capitalism could develop without opposition. They were easily exploited to the limit. They would work long hours amidst almost intolerable conditions. Whoever wishes to learn of the deplorable state of the proletariat during the early days of modern industry has but to read Frederich Engles' classic work on the working-class of England.

5. The Advance of the Wage-Earning Proletariat.

At the time of the beginning of modern industry the term proletariat implied absolute degeneracy. And there are persons who believe this is still the case. But even in the earliest days there was the beginning of a great gulf between the working-class proletariat and the slum proletariat.

The slum proletariat has always been the same, whether in modern London or ancient Rome.

The modern laboring proletariat is an absolutely unique phenomenon.

Between these two there is, first of all, the difference that lies in the fact that the first is a parasite and the second the most important root of modern social life. Far from receiving alms, the modern working proletarians support the whole structure of our society. At first, to be sure, they do not perceive this, but sooner or later they discover that instead of receiving their bread from the capitalist they furnish him his.

From house-servants and apprentices, on the other hand, the working proletarians distinguish themselves by the fact that they do not live and work with their exploiters. The personal relations that formerly bound them to their employers have disappeared.

On the other hand, the modern working-man does not envy and imitate the rich, as did the poor of pre-capitalist days. He hates them as enemies and despises them as idlers.

At first this feeling exhibits itself sporadically. But as soon as the workers discover that their interests are common, that they are all opposed to the exploiter, it takes the form of great organizations and open battles against the exploiting class. The sense of power that goes with class-consciousness means the regeneration of the working-class. It raises this class forever above the level of the parasitic poor.

All the conditions of modern production tend to increase the solidarity of the laboring classes. In the Middle Ages each artisan produced a finished product; he was industrially almost independent. Today it often takes scores, or even hundreds, to produce a finished product. Thus does industry teach co-operation.

Perhaps modern uniformity of conditions is even more effective in this direction than the necessity for co-operation. In the Medieval gilds there were the beginning of internationalism, but the various trades were sharply divided. Among the menial, as we have seen, divisions in rank were endless. But in the modern factory there are practically no gradations. All the employes work under nearly the same conditions, and the individual laborer is powerless to change them. Under the influence of machinery, moreover, the distinctions among the trades are rapidly disappearing. This is indicated by the fact that apprenticeships are constantly being shortened. Whole trades are often rendered unnecessary by some new invention, and those employed in them are forced to turn to another form of labor. This tends more and more to make an individual worker forget his craft and fight for his entire class.

Uprisings against employers are nothing new. They occurred in plenty during the Middle Ages. But only during the nineteenth century did these uprisings attain the character of a class-struggle. And thus this great conflict has taken on a higher purpose than the righting of temporary wrongs; the labor movement has become a revolutionary movement.

6.   The Conflict Between the Elevating and Degrading Tendencies Which Affect the Proletariat.

The elevation of the working-class is a necessary and inevitable process.   But it is neither peaceful nor regular.   The tendency of the capitalist system is, as we have shown in Chapter II, to degrade the proletariat ever more and more. The moral regeneration of the working-class is possible only in opposition to this tendency and its representatives, the capitalists.   It cannot come about except through the new tendency developed in the working-class by the modern conditions of labor.   But the two tendencies, the one upward and the other downward, vary constantly in different places and at different periods. They depend on the condition of the market, the organization of industry, the development of machinery, the insight of the capitalists and workers, etc., etc.   All of these conditions vary from year to year in all the numerous branches of industry.

But fortunately for human development there comes a time in the history of every section of the proletariat when the elevating tendencies gain the upper hand.   And when they have once wakened full class-consciousness in any group of workers, the consciousness of solidarity with all the members of the working-class, the consciousness of the strength that is born of union; as soon as any group has recognized that it is essential to society and that it dare hope for better things in the future,—then it is well nigh impossible to shove that group back into the degenerate mass of beings whose opposition to the

system under which they suffer takes no other
form than that of unreasoned hate.

7. Philanthropy and Labor Legislation.

If every section of the proletariat had been
dependent on its own efforts, the uplifting process would have begun much later and been much
slower and more painful than it actually was.
Without help many a division of the proletariat
now occupying an honorable position would not
have been at all able to overcome the difficulties
that are inherent in all beginnings. Aid came
from many an upper social rank, from the upper
ranks of the proletariat as well as from the
property-holding classes. The assistance rendered by the latter of these was of no slight
value in the early days of capitalist large production.

During the Middle Ages poverty was so slight
that public and private benevolence sufficed to
deal with it. It presented no problem for society
to solve; in so far as it gave occasion for reflec-
tion it was only the subject of pious contem-
plation; it was looked upon as a visitation from
heaven, intended either to punish the wicked or
try the godly. To the rich it furnished an opportunity to exercise their virtue.

With the growth of the capitalist system, however, the number of the unemployed increased,
and poverty assumed tremendous proportions.
The spectacle of a large pauper class, which was
as novel as it was dangerous, drew upon it the
attention of all thoughtful and kindly disposed
persons. Primitive means for the distribution

of charity proved inadequate. To care for all
the poor was soon felt to be a work that greatly
exceeded the powers of the community. Then
there arose a new problem: how to abolish poverty? A great many solutions were offered.
These ranged from schemes to get rid of the
poor by hanging or deportation to elaborate plans
for communistic colonies. The latter met with
great applause among people of culture, but the
former were the only suggestions ever really
tried.

By degrees, however, the question of poverty
took on a new aspect. The capitalistic system of
production developed rapidly and finally became
the controlling one. As this development went
on, the problem of poverty ceased to exist for the
thinkers in the capitalist class. Capitalist production rests upon the proletariat; to put an end
to the latter were to render the former impossible.
Colossal poverty is the foundation of colossal
wealth; he who would eliminate the poverty of
the masses assails the wealth of the few. Accordingly, whoever attempts to remedy the poverty of the workers is pronounced "an enemy of
law and order."

True enough, neither fear nor compassion has
ceased, even under this changed aspect of things,
to be felt in capitalist circles, and to tell in favor
of the proletariat. For poverty is a source of
danger to the whole social fabric; it breeds pesti-
lence and crime. Accordingly a few of the more
clear-headed and humane among the ruling
classes are willing to do something for the working-class; but to the bulk of them, who neither

dare, nor can afford, to break with their own class, the problem can no longer be that of the abolition of the protetariat. At best they cannot go beyond the elevation of the proletarian. The proletariat is by all means to continue, able to work and satisfied with its condition.

Within these bounds, of course, philanthropy can manifest itself in manifold ways. Most of its methods are either wholly useless or calculated only to give temporary aid in isolated cases.

There is, however, one notable exception to this generalization. I refer to labor legislation. When, during the first decades of the nineteenth century, capitalist production on a large scale made its entry into England and was there accompanied by all the horrors which it can produce under the worst conditions, the wisest among the philanthropists arrived at the conviction that there was but one thing able to check the degeneration of the workers in the industries affected. They immediately began to propose laws for the protection of the workers, at least for the protection of the most helpless among them, the women and children.

The capitalists engaged in large production in England did not at that time constitute the ruling section of the capitalist class, as they do today. Many economic, as well as political, interests among the other sections—especially the small producers and landlords—spoke in favor of limiting the powers of the large capitalists over their workmen. The movement in this direction was favored also by the consideration that unless the large capitalists were restrained, the working class, which was the foundation of English industry, would inevitably perish. This was a consideration which could not fail to influence every member of the ruling class intelligent enough to see further than his own immediate interests. Added to this there was the support of a few large capitalists who realized that they had sufficient means to adapt themselves to the proposed laws and who saw that their less wealthy competitors would be ruined by them. In spite of all this, and notwithstanding the fact that the working-class itself set in motion a powerful movement in favor of factory laws, it took a hard fight to obtain the first slight factory legislation and subsequently to extend it.

Slight though these first conquests seemed, they were, nevertheless, sufficient to awaken out of their lethargy those ranks of the proletariat in whose behalf they were passed and to arouse in them the upward tendencies inherent in their social position. Indeed, even before the movement had achieved any victory, the struggle was enough to reveal to the proletarians how important they were and what a power they wielded. These early struggles shook them up, imparted to them self-consciousness and self-respect, put an end to their despair, and set up before them a goal beyond their immediate future.

Another, and extremely important, means of improving the condition of the working-class is the public schools. Their influence cannot be overestimated. Nevertheless their effect in the direction of elevating the proletariat is inferior to that of thorough-going factory laws.

The more fully the capitalist system develops, the more large production crowds out inferior forms or changes their character, the more imperative does the strengthening of factory laws become. It becomes necessary to extend them, not only to all branches of large industry, but to home industry and agriculture, as well. In the same measure as the importance of these laws increases there grows also the influence of large capitalists in modern society. Property-owners who are not industrial capitalists—landlords, small manufacturers, shop-keepers, etc.—become infected with capitalist modes of thought. The thinkers and statesmen of the bourgeoisie, formerly its far-sighted leaders, sink to the role of mere defenders of the capitalist class.

The devastation of the working-class by capitalist production is so shocking that only the most shameless and greedy capitalists dare to refuse a certain amount of statutory protection to labor. But for any important labor measure, the eight-hour law, for example, there will be found few supporters among the property-holding class. Capitalist philanthropy becomes constantly more timid; it tends more and more to leave to the workers themselves the struggle for their protection. The modern struggle for the eight-hour day bears a very different aspect from the one which was carried on in England fifty years ago for the ten-hour day. The property-holding politicians who are advocating the modern measure are moved, not by philanthropy, but by the necessity of yielding to their working-class constituents. The struggle

for labor legislation is becoming more and more
a class-struggle between proletarians and capitalists. On the continent of Europe and in the
United States, where the struggle for labor laws
commenced much later than in England, it bore
this character from the start. The proletariat has
nothing more to hope for from the property-
holding classes in its endeavor to raise itself. It
now depends wholly upon its own efforts.

8. The Labor Union Movement.

Struggles between laborers and exploiters are
nothing new. Extremely bitter and protracted
ones occurred toward the end of the Middle
Ages between apprentices and masters. As early
as the fifteenth century, masters here and there
would seek to escape from work by increasing the
number of their apprentices. On the other hand
they made it more and more difficult for any but
their sons to become masters. Gradually the
family relation between master and man was
loosened, and the modern division into classes
had begun.

As soon as the master began to play the part
of modern capitalist, conflicts were inevitable.
And in one respect the apprentices were in a good
position to assert themselves. In each city they
were well organized. Each gild included all the
apprentices in a particular trade; it controlled
absolutely the supply of labor so far as that trade
was concerned. When the time of conflict arrived, it could use with tremendous effectiveness
the weapons which have become so familiar in
modern times, the strike and the boycott.

All the increasing power of the modern state was called into action to teach the unruly apprentices their place. The suppression of the working-class has been from the beginning the chief function of the state, and in these early days it performed this function with terrible effect. But all its efforts did not succeed in putting an end to the trouble. Denied the right of organization, the apprentices formed secret unions and maintained them in the face of frightful persecutions.

But what the state could not accomplish was accomplished by industrial evolution. After the close of the Middle Ages, particularly during the eighteenth century, manufacturing was becoming an increasingly important feature of the industrial world. Before the introduction of machinery, employes in factories had the advantages neither of the Medieval system of industry nor of the modern. They lived in large towns and were often of various races. More than this, different degrees of skill were demanded for different occupations. For all of these reasons they found it difficult to organize. Their only advantage lay in the fact that their work did require skill. They were not compelled to compete against the entire mass of the unemployed.

Only the introduction of machinery altered this last condition. It made the whole mass of the unemployed serviceable to capitalism and threw even proletarian women and children upon the labor market.

Since the introduction of machinery the transformation of industry has proceeded at an unprecedented pace. To be sure, mechanical methods were not immediately introduced into all industrial branches. In some branches even the old handicraft methods have survived. Such survivals, however, instead of tending to prolong former conditions, usually lead, as has been the case in the tailoring industry, to sweat-shop labor. That is, they produce the class of laborers least able to resist their masters.

But the tendency is to introduce machines into all departments of industry. The effect on the power of resistance developed in the working-class is of the utmost importance. In the first place this change tends to divide the workers into two classes, skilled and unskilled. The former class includes all whose work requires any special degree of skill or efficiency. The latter includes, of course, all those who perform such labor as can be done by any one having the requisite strength. The characteristic mark of members of this latter class is to be found in the fact that they can be easily replaced.

It was naturally the skilled workers who began the struggle for better conditions. The fact that it was difficult to find substitutes for them in case of a strike gave them an important strategic advantage. Their position was not unlike that of the medieval apprentices, and in many respects their unions were natural descendants of the gilds.

But if modern skilled laborers inherited certain advantages from their predecessors, they also took over from them one tendency which has done great harm to the modern labor movement. This is the tendency to separate the various crafts. Naturally those in the best position to fight have won for themselves superior advantages and have come to look upon themselves as an aristocracy of labor. Looking only at their own interest, they have been content to rise at the expense of their less fortunate comrades.

Far-sighted politicians and industrial leaders have not been slow to take advantage of this condition. Today the worst enemies of the working-class are not the stupid, reactionary statesmen who hope to keep down the labor movement through openly repressive measures. Its worst enemies are the pretended friends who encourage craft unions, and thus attempt to cut off the skilled trades from the rest of their class. They are trying to turn the most efficient division of the proletarian army against the great mass, against those whose position as unskilled workers makes them least capable of defense.

But sooner or later the aristocratic tendency of even the most highly skilled class of laborers will be broken. As mechanical production advances, one craft after another is tumbled into the abyss of common labor. This fact is constantly teaching even the most effectively organized divisions that in the long run their position is dependent upon the strength of the working-class as a whole. They come to the conclusion that it is a mistaken policy to attempt to rise on the shoulders of those who are sinking in a quicksand. They come to see that the struggles of other divisions of the proletariat are by no means foreign to them.

At the same time one division of the unskilled after another rises out of its stupid lethargy or mere purposeless discontent. This is in part a natural consequence of the successes achieved by the skilled laborers. The direct results of the activities of the unskilled proletarians may seem unimportant, nevertheless it is these activities that bring about the moral regeneration of this division of the working-class.

Thus there has gradually formed from skilled and unskilled workers a body of proletarians who are in the movement of labor, or the labor movement. It is the part of the proletariat which is fighting for the interests of the whole class, its church militant, as it were. This division grows at the expense both of the "aristocrats of labor" and of the common mob which still vegetates, helpless and hopeless. We have already seen that the laboring proletariat is constantly increasing; we know, further, that it tends more and more to set the pace in thought and feeling for the other working classes. We now see that in this growing mass of workers the militant division increases not only absolutely, but relatively. No matter how fast the proletariat may grow, this militant division of it grows still faster.

But it is precisely this militant proletariat which is the most fruitful recruiting ground for socialism. The socialist movement is nothing more than the part of this militant proletariat which has become conscious of its goal. In fact, these two, socialism and the militant proletariat, tend constantly to become identical. In Germany and Austria their identity is already an accomplished fast.

9. The Political Struggle.

The original organizations of the proletariat were modeled after those of the medieval apprentices. In like manner the first weapons of the modern labor movement were those inherited from a previous age, the strike and the boycott.

But these methods are insufficient for the modern proletariat. The more completely the various divisions of which it is made up unite into a single working-class movement, the more must its struggles take on a political character. Every class-struggle is a political struggle.

Even the bare requirements of the industrial struggle force the workers to make political demands. We have seen that the modern state regards it as its principal function to make the effective organization of labor impossible. Secret organizations are inefficient substitutes for open ones. The more the proletariat develops, the more it needs freedom to organize.

But this freedom is not alone sufficient if the proletariat is to have adequate organizations. The apprentices and journeymen of previous periods found it easy to act together. The various cities were industrially independent. In any given city the number of those engaged in any trade was comparatively small. They usually lived on one street and spent their leisure time at the same tavern. Each one was personally acquainted with all the rest.

Today conditions are radically different. In

every industrial center there are gathered thousands of working-men. A single individual can know personally only a few of his comrades. To make this great mass feel its common interests, to induce it to act as one in an organization, it is necessary to have means of communicating with large numbers. A free press and the right of assemblage are absolutely essential.

The free press is made especially necessary by the development of modern means of communication. It is possible now for a capitalist to import strike-breakers from far-lying districts. Unless the workers can organize unions covering the entire nation, or even the entire civilized world, they are powerless. But this cannot be done without the aid of the press.

On this account, wherever the working-class has endeavored to improve its economic position it has made political demands, especially demands for a free press and the right of assemblage. These privileges are to the proletariat the prerequisites of life; they are the light and air of the labor movement. Whoever attempts to deny them, no matter what his pretensions, is to be reckoned among the worst enemies of the working-class.

Occasionally some one has attempted to oppose the political struggle to the economic, and declared that the proletariat should give its exclusive attention either to the one or the other. The fact is that the two cannot be separated. The economic struggle demands political rights, and these will not fall from heaven. To secure and maintain them, the most vigorous political action is necessary. The political struggle is, on the other hand, in the last analysis, an economic struggle. Often, in fact, it is directly and openly economic, as when it deals with tariff and factory laws. The political struggle is merely a particular form of the economic struggle, in fact, its most inclusive and vital form.

The interest of the working-class is not limited to the laws which directly affect it; the great majority of laws touch its interests to some extent. Like every other class, the working-class must strive to influence the state authorities, to bend them to its purposes.

Great capitalists can influence rulers and legislators directly, but the workers can do so only through parliamentary activity. It matters little whether a government be republican in name. In all parliamentary countries it rests with the legislative body to grant tax levies. By electing representatives to parliament, therefore, the working-class can exercise an influence over the governmental powers.

The struggle of all the classes which depend upon legislative action for political influence is directed, in the modern state, on the one hand toward an increase in the power of the parliament (or congress), and on the other toward an increase in their own influence within the parliament. The power of parliament depends on the energy and courage of the classes behind it and on the energy and courage of the classes on which its will is to be imposed. The influence of a class within a parliament depends, in the first place, on the nature of the electoral law in force. It is dependent, further, upon the influence of the class in question among the voters, and, lastly, upon its aptitude for parliamentary work.

A word must be added on this last point. The bourgeoisie, with all sorts of talent at its command, has hitherto been able to manipulate parliaments to its own purpose. Therefore, small capitalists and farmers have in large numbers lost all faith in legislative action. Some of these have declared in favor of the substitution of direct legislation for legislation by representatives; others have denounced all forms of political activity. This may sound very revolutionary, but in reality it indicates nothing but the political bankruptcy of the classes involved.

The proletariat is, however, more favorably situated in regard to parliamentary activity. We have already seen how the modern method of production reacts on the intellectual life of the proletariat, how it has awakened in them a thirst for knowledge and given them an understanding of great social problems. So far as their attitude toward politics is concerned, they are raised far above the farmers and small capitalists. It is easier for them to grasp party principles and act on them uninfluenced by personal and local motives. Their conditions of life, moreover, make it possible for them to act together in great numbers for a common end. Their regular forms of activity accustom them to rigid discipline. Their unions are to them an excellent parliamentary school; they afford opportunities for training in parliamentary law and public speaking.

The proletariat is, therefore, in a position to form an independent party. It knows how to control its representatives. Moreover, it finds in its own ranks an increasing number of persons well fitted to represent it in legislative halls.

Whenever the proletariat engages in parliamentary activity as a self-conscious class, parliamentarism begins to change its character. It ceases to be a mere tool in the hands of the bourgeoisie. This very participation of the proletariat proves to be the most effective means of shaking up the hitherto indifferent divisions of the proletariat and giving them hope and confidence. It is the most powerful lever that can be utilized to raise the proletariat out of its economic, social and moral degradation.

The proletariat has, therefore, no reason to distrust parliamentary action; on the other hand, it has every reason to exert all its energy to increase the power of parliaments in their relation to other departments of government and to swell to the utmost its own parliamentary representation. Besides freedom of the press and the right to organize, the universal ballot is to be regarded as one of the conditions prerequisite to a sound development of the proletariat.

10. The Labor Party.

In the first place the ballot was useful to the working-class only because it now and then made various sections of the bourgeoisie dependent on it for favors. In their internal struggles capitalist factions, as, for example, the industrial capitalists or the landlords, would offer advantages to the proletariat for the sake of securing its support. Though this procedure often resulted in valuable concessions, nevertheless so long as the working-class went no further in its political activities there was a definite limit to its possibilities.

The interests of the proletariat and the bourgeoisie are of so contrary a nature that in the long run they cannot be harmonized. Sooner or later in every capitalist country the participation of the working-class in politics must lead to the formation of an independent party, a labor party.

At what moment in its history the proletariat of any particular country will reach the point at which it is ready to take this step, depends chiefly upon its economic development. In some degree, also, it depends upon two other conditions, the insight of the working-class into the political and economic situation and the attitude of the bourgeois parties toward one another.

But an independent labor party is bound to come sooner or later. And, once formed, such a party must have for its purpose the conquest of the government in the interest of the class which it represents. Economic development will lead naturally to the accomplishment of this purpose. The time and manner of its accomplishment may vary in different lands, but there can be no doubt as to the final victory of the proletariat. For this class grows constantly in moral and political power as well as in numbers. The class-struggle widens its view and teaches it solidarity and discipline. In capitalist countries it tends constantly to become the only working class, hence the class upon which all others are dependent. On the other hand, the classes opposed to the proletariat diminish constantly in numbers and lose visibly in moral and political power. In industry they become, not only superfluous, but often actually detrimental.

Under these circumstances there can be no doubt as to which side will eventually be victorious. Long ago the possessing classes were seized with fear of their approaching fate.

But the proletariat, as the lowest of the exploited classes—the slum-proletariat is not exploited—cannot use its power, as the other classes have done, to shift the burden of exploitation to other shoulders. It must put an end to its own exploitation and in the same act to all exploitation. The root of exploitation, however, is to be found in private ownership of the means of production. The proletariat can do away with the former only by destroying the latter. If the propertyless condition of the proletariat makes possible its winning over to the abolition of this form of private property, its exploitation will compel it to abolish exploitation and to substitute co-operative for capitalist production.

But we have seen that this cannot come about so long as commodity production remains supreme. In order to substitute co-operative for capitalist production it is absolutely necessary to replace production for the market with produc tion for the community and under the control of the community. Socialist production is, therefore, the natural result of, a victory of the proletariat. If the working-class did not make use of its mastery over the machinery of government to introduce the socialist system of production, the logic of events would finally call some such system into being—but only after a useless waste of energy and time. But socialist production must, and will, come. Its victory will have become inevitable as soon as that of the proletariat has become inevitable. The working-class will naturally strive to put an end to exploitation, and this it can do only through socialist production.

Thus it appears that wherever an independent labor party is formed it must sooner or later exhibit socialist tendencies; if not socialist in the beginning, it must become so in the end.

We have now examined the chief recruiting grounds of socialism. Our results may be summed up as follows: the militant, politically self-conscious divisions of the industrial proletariat furnish the power which is behind the socialist movement; but the more the influence of the proletariat affects the ways of thinking and feeling in vogue among allied social groups, the more will these, also, be drawn into the movement.

11. The Labor Movement and Socialism.

In the beginning socialists were slow to recognize the part which the militant proletariat is called upon to play in the socialist movement. It could not be otherwise, in the nature of things, so long as there was no militant proletariat. And socialism is older than the class-struggle of the proletariat. It dates back to the time of the first appearance of the proletariat on a large scale. It was not until much later that the proletarians showed the first stirrings of independent life. The first root of socialism was the sympathy of upper-class philanthropists with the poor and miserable. The early socialists were merely the bravest and most far-sighted of these philanthropists. They saw clearly that the existence of the proletariat was a natural result of the private ownership of the means of production, and they did not hesitate to draw the logical conclusions from their observation. Socialism was the deepest and most splendid expression of bourgeois philanthropy.

There were no class interests to which the socialists of that day could appeal; they were forced to turn to the sympathy and enthusiasm of upper-class idealists. They attempted to secure support by means of alluring descriptions of a socialist commonwealth, on the one side, and persistent representations of the prevailing misery, on the other. The rich and mighty were to be persuaded to furnish means for a thoroughgoing relief of misery and the institution of an ideal society. As is well known, these philanthropic socialists waited in vain for the noblemen and millionaires whose magnanimity was to save the race.

During the first decades of the nineteenth century the proletariat began to show signs of an independent life. During the thirties a vigorous labor movement got under way in France and England.

But the socialists did not understand it. They thought it impossible for the poor and ignorant proletarians to attain to the moral elevation and social power requisite for the realization of the socialist plans. But distrust was not their only feeling toward the labor movement. This new phenomenon was inconvenient to them; it threatened to rob them of their most effective argument. For the bourgeois socialists' only hope of winning over the sensitive capitalist lay in being able to show him that every attempt to alleviate misery and elevate the poor was doomed to failure by the conditions of modern society and that, consequently, it was impossible for the proletarians to rise through their own efforts. But the labor movement proceeded upon premises absolutely opposed to this line of argument. Another fact tended to bring about the same result. The class-struggle naturally embittered the bourgeoisie against the proletariat. In the eyes of the capitalists the working-class were transformed from pitiful unfortunates who needed help into a pack of miscreants who should be subdued and kept down. Sympathy for the poor and miserable, which had been the chief root of socialism, began to wither. The teachings of socialism came to appear to the terror-stricken bourgeoisie as a dangerous weapon which might fall into the hands of the mob and bring about unspeakable harm. In short, the stronger the labor movement appeared the more

difficult became socialist propaganda among the
ruling classes, and the more well-defined became
the opposition of these classes to the socialist
movement.

So long as socialists were of the opinion that
the means of attaining the objects of socialism
must come from the capitalist class, they were
compelled, not only to look with suspicion upon
the labor movement, but often to assume an attitude of direct opposition to it. As a result they
came to regard the class-struggle as the enemy
of socialism.

This naturally reacted upon the laboring
classes, tended to make of them enemies of
socialism. The ambitious, struggling proletarians discovered nothing but opposition among
the socialists and nothing but discouragement in
the socialist teachings. As a result, there was
born among them a distrust of the whole body
of socialist doctrine. This feeling was favored
by the ignorance even of the militant proletariat
at the beginning of the labor movement. The
narrowness of their view made it impossible for
them to grasp the purposes of socialism, and as
yet they were unconscious of their economic
position and of the tasks which confronted their
class. They felt only an indefinite class instinct
which taught them to distrust everything that
had its origin in the capitalist class. Under the
circumstances they were naturally as much opposed to socialism as to any other form of
bourgeois philanthropy.

Among certain groups of working-men, especially in England, distrust of socialism took

deep root at this time. It is partly because of
this that until recently England has been comparatively unaffected by the socialist movement.

But no matter how wide might grow the
chasm between socialism and the militant proletariat, socialist philosophy is so adequate to the
needs of thinking proletarians that the best
minds in the working-class, as soon as they had
opportunity, willingly turned to it. Then the
bourgeois socialist came under the influence of
proletarian thinking. The new, proletarian
socialists took little account of the capitalist
class. They hated it and were fighting against
it. In their hands the peaceful socialism which
was to save the race through the intervention of
the best elements in the upper classes was transformed into a violent revolutionary socialism
which was to depend for its support upon proletarian fists.

But even this movement, though essentially
proletarian in its origin, had no understanding
of the labor movement; it stood in opposition to
the class-struggle in its highest form, that is, the
political struggle. In the nature of the case it
was impossible for it to transcend the theories
of the utopians. At best a proletarian can do no
more than appropriate for his own purposes a
part of the learning of the bourgeois world. He
lacks the leisure necessary to carry independent
scientific investigation beyond the point reached
by bourgeois thinkers. Therefore primitive
working-class socialism bore all the marks of
utopianism. It had no notion of the economic
evolution which is creating the material ele-

ments of socialist production and, by means of a
long struggle, is training the class that is to
vitalize these elements and develop from them
a new society. Like the utopians, the early proletarian socialists looked upon society as a building which could be constructed arbitrarily according to a preconceived plan if one had only
the required space and materials. They trusted
themselves to furnish the power both to build
and to preserve this structure. As to the materials and place, they did not expect these from
the bounty of some millionaire or nobleman; the
revolution was to be sufficient to tear down the
old structure, to overpower its defenders, and
give the discoverers of the new plan an opportunity to build the new structure, the socialist
commonwealth.

In this course of reasoning there was no place
for the class-struggle. The proletarian utopians
found the misery in which they lived so bitter
that they were impatient for its immediate removal. Even if they had thought it possible for
the class-struggle to raise the proletariat gradually, and thus fit them for the further development of society, this process would have seemed
to them much too tedious and complex. But
they did not believe in this gradual elevation.
They stood at the beginning of the labor movement. The group of proletarians who partici-
pated in it were few, and among these only a
still smaller number saw beyond their temporary
interests. To train the great mass of the population in socialist ways of thinking seemed hopeless. The most that could be expected of this

mass was a violent outbreak which might destroy the existing order and thus clear the way for socialism. The worse the condition of the masses, thought these primitive socialists, the nearer must be the moment when their misery would become unbearable and they would rise and topple over the social structure which oppressed them. A struggle for the gradual elevation of the working-class seemed not only hopeless, but harmful. For any slight improvement that might be achieved could only tend to postpone the moment of their uprising and, therefore, the moment of permanent release from misery. Every form of the class-struggle which was not aimed at the immediate overthrow of the existing order, that is, every serious, efficient sort of effort, seemed to the early socialist as nothing more nor less than a betrayal of humanity. It is now more than fifty years since this way of looking at things made its appearance. Its best expression it received, probably, in the works of Wilhelm Weitling. Even today it has not died out. The tendency toward it appears in every division of the working-class which begins to take its place in the ranks of the militant proletariat. It appears in every land where the proletariat becomes for the first time conscious of its degraded condition and imbued with socialistic notions, without at the same time having reached a clear insight into social laws and gained confidence in its ability to carry on a protracted struggle. And since new divisions of the proletariat are constantly rising out of the depths into which economic development has thrust them, this primitive socialist way of thinking may be expected continually to make its reappearance. It is a children's disease which threatens every young socialist movement which has not got beyond utopianism.

At present this sort of socialistic thinking is called anarchy, but it is not necessarily connected with anarchism. It has its origin, not in clear understanding, but rather in mere instinctive opposition to the existing order. Therefore it may be connected with the most varied theoretical points of view. But it is true that the rude and violent socialism of the primitive proletarians is often associated with the refined and peaceable anarchy of the small bourgeois. With all their differences these two have one thing in common, hatred of the protracted class-struggle, especially of its highest form, the political struggle.

The proletarian utopians were no more able than their forerunners to overcome the opposition between socialism and the labor movement. It is true that conditions occasionally compelled them to take active part in the class-struggle. But they were too illogical to see the connection between socialism and the labor movement. Therefore their activity merely resulted in the crowding out of the former by the latter. It is well known that the early anarchist-socialist movement sank sooner or later either into pure-and-simple craft unionism or mere co-operative communism.

12. The Socialist Party—Union of the Labor Movement and Socialism.

If the socialist movement and the labor movement were ever to become one it was necessary for socialism to be raised beyond the utopian point of view. To accomplish this was the illustrious work of Marx and Engels. In their Communist Manifesto, published in 1847, they laid the scientific foundation of modern socialism. They transformed the beautiful dream of well-meaning enthusiasts into the goal of a great and earnest struggle, they proved it to be the natural result of economic development. To the militant proletariat they gave a clear conception of their historical function, and placed them in a position to proceed toward their great goal with as much speed and as few sacrifices as possible. The socialists are no longer expected to discover a new and free social order; all they have to do is discover the elements of such an order in existing society. They need no longer attempt to bring to the proletariat salvation from above. On the other hand, it becomes their duty to support the working-class in its constant struggle by encouraging its political and economic institutions. It must do all in its power to hasten the day when the working-class will be able to save itself. To give to the class-struggle of the proletariat the most effective form, this is the function of the Socialist Party.

The teaching of Marx and Engels gave to the class-struggle of the proletariat an entirely new character. So long as socialist production is not kept consciously in view as its object, so long as the efforts of the militant proletariat do not extend beyond the framework of the existing method of production, the class-struggle seems to move forever in a circle. For the oppressive tendencies of the capitalist method of production are not done away with; at most they are only checked. Without cessation, new groups of the middle class are thrown into the proletariat. The desire for profits constantly threatens to bring to nought the achievements of the more favorably situated divisions of labor. Every reduction in the hours of labor becomes an excuse for the introduction of labor-saving machinery and for the intensification of labor. Every improvement in the organization of labor is answered with an improvement in the organization of capital. And all the time unemployment increases, crises become more serious, and the uncertainty of existence grows more unendurable. The elevation of the working-class brought about by the class-struggle is more moral than economic. The industrial conditions of the proletariat improve but slowly, if at all. But the self-respect of the proletarians mounts higher, as does also the respect paid them by the other classes of society. They begin to regard themselves as the equals of the upper classes and to compare the conditions of the other strata of society with their own. They make greater demands on society, demands for better clothes, better dwellings, greater knowledge and the education of their children. They wish to have some share in the achievements of modern civilization. And they feel with increasing keenness

every set-back, every new form of oppression.
This moral elevation of the proletariat is
identical with the increasing demands which it
makes on society. Moreover it advances more
rapidly than the conditions of labor which necessarily prevail under the present system of exploitation. The result of the class-struggle can,
therefore, be nothing else than increasing discontent among the proletarians. And therefore
the class-struggle appears purposeless so long as
it does not look beyond the present system of
production.

Only socialist production can put an end to
the disparity between the demands of the workers and the means of satisfying them. By doing
away with exploitation it would render impossible the luxuries of the exploiters and the natural
discontent of the exploited. With the removal
of the standard set by the rich the demands of
the workers would, of course, be measured by
the means at hand to satisfy them. We have
already seen how much the socialist method of
production would increase these means.

Perpetual discontent is unknown in communistic societies. In our capitalistic world it
results naturally from the distinction of classes
wherever the exploited feel themselves to be the
equals of the exploiters.

So long, therefore, as the class-struggle of the
proletariat was opposed to socialism, so long as
it did nothing beyond attempting to improve the
position of the proletariat within the framework
of existing society, it could not reach its goal.
But a great change came with the amalgamation

of socialism and the labor movement. Now the proletariat has a goal toward which it is struggling, which it comes nearer to with every battle. Now all features of the class-struggle have a meaning, even those that produce no immediately practical results. Every effort that preserves or increases the self-consciousness of the proletariat or its spirit of co-operation and discipline, is worth the making.

Many an apparent defeat is turned into a victory. Every unsuccessful strike, every labor law defeated, means a step toward the securing of a life worthy of human beings. Every political or industrial measure which has reference to the proletariat has a good effect. Whether it be friendly or unfriendly, matters not, so long as it tends to stir up the working-class. From now on the militant proletariat is no longer like an army fighting hard to defend positions already won; now it must become clear to the dullest onlooker that it is an irresistible conqueror.

13. The International Character of the Socialist Movement.

The founders of modern socialism recognized from the beginning the international character which the labor movement tends everywhere to assume. So they naturally attempted to give their movement an international basis.

International commerce is inevitably connected with the capitalist system of production. The development of capitalism out of early, simple production of commodities is most intimately connected with the growth of world-commerce. But world-commerce is impossible without peaceful intercourse among the various nations. It requires that a foreign merchant be protected equally with a native.

The development of international commerce raises the merchant to a high position in our society. His way of looking at things begins to influence society as a whole. But the merchant has always been an unsettled person; his motto has ever been, Where I fare well, there is my home. Thus in proportion to the extension of world-commerce and capitalist production there develop international tendencies in bourgeois society.

The capitalist system of production, however, develops the most remarkable contradictions. Hand in hand with the movement toward international brotherhood goes a tendency to emphasize international differences. Commerce demands peace, but competition leads to war. If, in each country, the different capitalists and classes are in a state of war, so are the capitalist classes of the various countries. Each nation tries to extend the markets for its own goods by crowding out the goods of other nations. The more complex becomes international commerce, the more essential international peace, the fiercer grows the competitive struggle and the greater the danger of conflicts between nations. The closer the international relations which are developed, the louder swells the demand for attention to separate national interests. The more urgent the need of peace, the greater the danger of war. These apparently impossible antitheses correspond exactly to the character of capitalist production. They lie hidden in the simple production of commodities, but only capitalist production develops them till they become intolerable. That it develops at the same time the necessity of peace and the tendency toward war is only one of the contradictions which will bring about the destruction of the capitalist system.

The proletariat has not assumed the inconsistent attitude with regard to this matter that is characteristic of the other classes. The more the working-class develops and becomes independent, the clearer becomes the fact that it is influenced by only one of the opposing tendencies which we have just observed in the capitalist system. The capitalist system, by expropriating the worker, has freed him from the soil. He has now no settled home, and therefore no country. Like the merchant, he can take for his motto, Where I fare well, there is my home. Even the medieval apprentices extended their wanderings to foreign lands, and the beginning of an international relation was the result. But what were these wanderings in comparison with those made possible by modern means of travel? And the apprentice journeyed with the intention of returning to his home; the modern proletarian journeys with his wife and family in order to settle wherever he finds conditions most favorable. He is not a tourist, but a nomad.

The merchant in a foreign country depends upon his government for the support which is necessary to successful competition. He appreciates his country; often enough, in fact, he becomes the most confirmed among the jingos. It is different with the proletarian. At home he has not been spoiled by government protection of his interests. And in foreign lands, at least in such as are civilized, he has no need of protection. On the contrary, the new land is usually one in which the laws and their administration are more favorable to the worker than those of his original home. And his co-workers have no motive for depriving him of what little protection he can get from the law in his struggle against his exploiter. Their interest lies rather in increasing his ability to withstand the common enemy.

Very differently from the apprentice or the merchant is the modern proletarian torn loose from the soil. He becomes a citizen of the world; the whole world is his home.

No doubt this world-citizenship is a great hardship for the workers in countries where the standard of living is high and the conditions of labor are comparatively good. In such countries, naturally, immigration will exceed emigration. As a result the laborers with the higher standard of living will be hindered in their class-struggle by the influx of those with a lower standard and less power of resistance.

Under certain circumstances this sort of competition, like that of the capitalists, may lead to a new emphasis on national lines, a new hatred of foreign workers on the part of the native born. But the conflict of nationalities, which is perpetual among the capitalists, can be only temporary among the proletarians. For sooner or later the workers will discover that the immigration of cheap labor-power from the more backward to the more advanced countries, is as inevitable a result of the capitalist system as the introduction of machinery or the forcing of women into industry.

In still another way does the labor movement of an advanced country suffer under the influence of the backward conditions of other lands. The high degree of exploitation endured by the proletariat of the economically undeveloped nations becomes an excuse for the capitalists of the more highly developed ones for opposing any movement in the direction of higher wages or better conditions.

In more than one way, then, it is borne in upon the workers of each nation that their success in the class-struggle is dependent on the progress of the working-class of other nations. For a time this may turn them against foreign workers, but finally they come to see that there is only one effective means of removing the hindering influence of backward nations: *to do away with the backwardness itself*. German workers have every reason to co-operate with the Slavs and Italians in order that these may secure higher wages and a shorter working-day; the English workers have the same interest in relation to the Germans, and the Americans in relation to Europeans in general.

The dependence of the proletariat of one land on that of another leads inevitably to a joining of forces by the militant proletarians of various lands.

The survivals of national seclusion and national hatred which the proletariat took over from the bourgeoisie, disappear steadily. The working-class is freeing itself from national prejudices. Working-men learn more and more to see in the foreign laborer a fellow-fighter, a comrade.

The strongest bonds of international solidarity, naturally, are those which bind groups of proletarians, which, though of different nationalities, have the same purposes and use the same methods to accomplish them.

How necessary is the international union of the crass-struggles of the proletariat, as soon as they extend beyond a certain limit in purpose and strength, was recognized in the beginning by the authors of the Communist Manifesto. This historic document is addressed to the proletarians of all lands and concludes by calling upon them to unite. And the organization which they had won over to the acceptance of the principles of the manifesto, and in the name of which it was issued, was international, the Society of Communists.

The defeats of the revolutionary movements of 1848 and 1849 put an end to this society, but with the re-awakening of the labor movement in the sixties it came to life again in the International Workingmen's Association (founded in 1864). This association had for its purpose, not only to arouse a feeling of solidarity in the proletarians of different lands, but also to give them a common goal and lead them toward it by a common route. The first of these purposes was gloriously fulfilled, but the second was fulfilled only in part. The International was to bring about the union of socialism and the militant proletariat in all lands. It declared that the emancipation of the working-class could be accomplished only by the workers themselves; that the political movement was only a means to this end, and that the proletariat could not emancipate itself so long as it remained dependent upon the monopolists of the means of production. Within the International opposition to these principles developed in proportion to the clearness with which they were seen to lead to modern socialism. At that time there was still a comparatively large number of bourgeois and proletarian utopians. These, together with the pure-and-simple unionists, dropped out of the International as soon as they understood its purpose. The fall of the Paris Commune, in 1871, and persecutions in various European countries, hastened its fall.

But the consciousness of international solidarity that had been generated could not be smothered.

Since then the ideas of the Communist Manifesto have taken hold of the militant proletariat of Europe and of many proletarian groups outside of Europe. Everywhere the class-struggle and the socialist movement have become one, or are in a fair way to do so. The principles, objects and means of the proletarian class-struggle tend everywhere to become the same. This in

itself has been sufficient to produce a feeling of
union among the socialistic labor movements of
different countries. Their international consciousness has constantly grown stronger, and it
needed only an external impulse to give to this
fact visible expression.

This came about, as is well known, in connection with the celebration of the hundredth an-
niversary of the storming of the Bastile, which
occurred at the International Congress of Paris
in 1889. Since then the international character
of the proletarian struggle has had a visible
symbol in the May Day celebration. It has been
strengthened, moreover, by regularly recurring
international congresses. These congresses are
made up, not of isolated enthusiasts, like the
bourgeois peace congresses, but of the representatives of millions of working men and women.
Every May Day shows in the most impressive
manner that it is the masses of industrial workers in all the great centers of population of all
civilized lands that feel in themselves the consciousness of the international solidarity of the
proletariat, that protest against war and declare
that national divisions are no longer divisions between peoples, but between exploiters.

Such a bridging of the chasm between the nations, such an international amalgamation of
great sections of the people of different lands,
the history of the world has never seen before.
This phenomenon appears the more imposing
when we remember that it has come into existence under the shadow of military armaments
which, on their part, also offer a spectacle the

like of which has never before been seen in the world.

14. The Socialist Party and the People.

The Socialist movement has, in the nature of things, been from the beginning international in its character. But in each country it has at the same time the tendency to become a national party. That is, it tends to become the representative, not only of the industrial wage-earners, but of all laboring and exploited classes, or, in other words, of the great majority of the population. We have already seen that the industrial proletariat tends to become the only working-class. We have pointed out, also, that the other working-classes are coming more and more to resemble the proletariat in the conditions of labor and way of living. And we have discovered that the proletariat is the only one among the working-classes that grows steadily in energy, in intelligence, and in clear consciousness of its purpose. It is becoming the center about which the disappearing survivals of the other working-classes group themselves. Its ways of feeling and thinking are becoming standard for the whole mass of non-capitalists, no matter what their status may be.

As rapidly as the wage-earners become the leaders of the people, the labor party becomes a people's party. When an independent craftsman feels like a proletarian, when he recognizes that he, or at any rate his children, will sooner or later be thrust into the proletariat, that there is no salvation for him except through the liberation of the proletariat—from that moment on he will see in the Socialist Party the natural representative of his interests.

We have already explained that he has nothing to fear from a socialist victory. In fact such a victory would be distinctly to his advantage, for it would usher in a society that would free all workers from exploitation and oppression and give them security and prosperity.

But the Socialist Party represents the interests of all non-capitalist classes, not only in the future, but in the present. The proletariat, as the lowest of the exploited strata, cannot free itself from exploitation and oppression without putting an end to all exploitation and oppression. It is, therefore, their sworn enemy, no matter in what form they may appear; it is the champion of all the exploited and oppressed.

We spoke above of the International. It is significant that the occasion for its founding was furnished by a demonstration in favor of the Poles, who had risen against the yoke of the Czar. It was characteristic, also, that the first address sent ont by the International was a letter of congratulation to President Lincoln in which this association of working-men expressed its sympathy with the abolition movement. And, finally, the International was the first organization existing in England, and the first counting Englishmen among its members, which took the part of the Irish who were oppressed by the English ruling class. Not one of these causes, that of the Poles, the Irish, or the African slaves, was directly connected with the class interests of the wage-earners.

We are told, it is true, that the socialist movement depends on the progress of economic development; that socialist production depends on the earliest possible crowding out of small industry. Socialism has, it is therefore thought, an interest in the disappearance of the independent craftsman, the small business man and the small farmer. It demands their ruin, therefore cannot work in their interest.

In answer to this there is the following to be said: The socialist movement does not create economic development; the crowding out of small industry will be taken care of without its help by the capitalist class. It is true that socialism has no reason for attempting to hinder this development. But to stop economic development would not be to serve the real interests of the small farmers and business men. For all attempts to this end must remain fruitless, if they do not cause positive harm. To propose to the independent craftsman or farmer measures by which their small concerns can once more be made profitable, would not be in any sense to serve their interests; the only effect would be to arouse illusions which could not be realized.

Furthermore, although the downfall of small production is inevitable, it is not necessarily accompanied by all the horrible circumstances which are usually connected with it. We have seen that the disappearance of small production is only the last act of a long drama. The previous acts were taken up by the painful degeneration of the small producer. But the socialist movement has not the slightest advantage to gain from this degeneration. On the contrary, its advantage lies all in the opposite direction. The more degraded the groups from which the proletariat is recruited the more difficult it is to elevate the recruits to the point at which they are willing and able to join the ranks of the militant proletariat. It is upon the extension of this division of the proletariat, however, that the size and strength of the socialist movement depend. The fewer the demands made upon society by the farmer or independent craftsman, the more accustomed he is to ceaseless labor, the less resistance he will be able to offer after he has fallen into the proletariat. To a certain extent the same causes which bring about the international solidarity of the workers lead to a solidarity with the classes wrom which the proletariat is recruited.

Of course if the sinking farmer or small business man attempts to keep his head above water at the cost of the working-class, if, for example, he tries to lower wages or hinder the organization of labor, then he will always be opposed by the proletariat and by the Socialist Party. On the other hand, the socialist movement does all in its power to support measures which are calculated to bring about, without injury to the working-class, an amelioration of conditions for the farmer and small business man.

This appears unmistakably in the nature of the immediate demands which the socialist parties of different lands make on their respective governments. Certain of these demands are purely industrial in their nature, designed especially to secure the protection of the wage-earner. But the majority are concerned with interests which the proletariat and the other groups of the laboring population have in common. These include demands for such reforms as an income tax, the initiative and referendum, freedom of press and speech, election of judges, etc.

Some of these demands are included in the platforms of bourgeois parties; others can, in the nature of the case, be formulated only by an anti-capitalistic organization. And no bourgeois party will fight for them with the same energy as the Socialist Party. For this is the only party that really has an interest in relieving non-capitalist classes of their burdens, educating their children, and elevating their lives in general.

Only measures of the sort proposed by the Socialist Party are calculated to improve the position of the small producers so far as it is possible to improve it under existing conditions. To assist them *as producers* by fortifying them in the retention of their outlived method of production, is impossible, for it is opposed to the course of economic development. It is equally impossible to make capitalists out of any considerable number of them. It is only *as consumers* that the mass of them can be helped at all. But it is precisely the parties most friendly to the small producers that cast upon them, as consumers, the heaviest burdens. These burdens are real, but the elevation of small production which is supposed to accompany them, is nothing more than empty pretense.

To assist the small producer in his character of

consumer, far from hindering economic development, is a means of promoting it. The better the position of the small farmer or small capitalist as consumer, the higher his standard of living, the greater his physical or intellectual demands, the sooner will he cease the struggle against industry on a large scale. If he is accustomed to a good living he will rebel against the privations incident to a protracted struggle, and will the sooner prefer to take his place with the proletariat. And he will not group himself with the most submissive members of this class to which he has joined himself. He will pass directly into the ranks of the militant, purposeful proletarians, and thus hasten the victory of the proletariat.

This victory will not be born out of degradation, as many have believed; no more out of the degradation of the small producers than out of that of the proletariat. Socialism has as much cause to oppose degradation on the one side as on the other, and it does so to the best of its ability. To strengthen the socialist movement, therefore, is to the interest, not only of the wage-earners, but of all sections of the population which live by work and not by exploitation.

The small business men and farmers have never, since the beginning of the modern state, been in a position to defend their interests as against the interests of the other classes. Today they are less able to do it than ever. In order to fight their battles, they are forced to unite with one or more of the other classes. The instincts bred by the ownership of property drive them into the arms of the capitalist parties; that is, into coalition with one of the various groups of great property-owners. The capitalist parties themselves seek this coalition, in part because they need votes, in part because of more profound reasons. They know that today the private property of the small producers is the strongest support of the principle of private ownership in general, and therefore of their whole system of exploitation. To the good of the small producer they are indifferent. They are quick to burden him as a consumer; so far as they are concerned, it makes no difference how far he is shoved down, so long as his small business does not perish utterly and he thus remains in the ranks of the property-owners. At the same time all the bourgeois parties are interested in capitalist exploitation, hence in the progress of economic development. They desire, indeed, to maintain the farmer and independent craftsman, but as a matter of fact they do everything in their power to extend the domain of industry on a large scale and thus to suppress all forms of small production.

Quite different is the relation between the small producer and the socialist movement. Even if socialism can do nothing to maintain small production, the small producer has nothing to fear from it. It is the capitalists, not the proletarians, who expropriate the farmer and craftsman. The victory of the proletariat is, as we have seen in the previous chapter, the only means of putting an end to this exploitation. As consumers, moreover, the independent small producers have the same interests as the proletarians. They have, therefore, every reason to protect their interests by joining the Socialist Party.

It is, of course, not to be expected that they will quickly recognize this fact. But the stampede of the farmers and small capitalists from the ranks of the bourgeois parties has already begun. And it is a stampede of most remarkable character, for it is the best and bravest who lead the way—not to desert the field of battle, but rather to escape from the petty strife for their miserable existence into the gigantic, world-moving struggle for the institution of a society which shall give to all its members opportunity to share in the great conquests of modern civilization, into the struggle for the emancipation of all civilized peoples, yes, of all humanity, from the bondage of a system which threatens to crush it.

The more unbearable the existing system of production, the more evidently it is discredited, and the more unable the ruling parties show themselves to remedy our disgraceful social ills, the more illogical and unprincipled these parties become and the more they resolve themselves into cliques of self-seeking politicians, the greater will be the numbers of those who stream from the non-proletarian classes into the Socialist Party and, hand in hand with the irresistibly advancing proletariat, follow its banner to victory and triumph.